Product Marketing

For Technology Companies

Product Marketing

For Technology Companies

Mark Butje

ELSEVIER
BUTTERWORTH-
HEINEMANN

AMSTERDAM • BOSTON • HEIDELBERG • LONDON • NEW YORK • OXFORD
PARIS • SAN DIEGO • SAN FRANCISCO • SINGAPORE • SYDNEY • TOKYO

Elsevier Butterworth-Heinemann
Linacre House, Jordan Hill, Oxford OX2 8DP
30 Corporate Drive, Burlington, MA 01803

British Library Cataloguing in Publication Data
A catalogue record for this book is available from the British Library

Library of Congress Cataloguing in Publication Data
A catalogue record for this book is available from the Library of Congress

ISBN   0 7506 5994 7

For information on all Elsevier Butterworth-Heinemann publications
visit our website at http://books.elsevier.com

Typeset by Integra Software Services Pvt. Ltd, Pondicherry, India
www.integra-india.com
Printed and bound in Great Britian

Contents

Figures

About the author

Mark Butje has over 20 years of experience working in the IT and Telecommunications industry in various areas: from software and database design to training, product marketing and marketing management, and from marketing strategy development to day-to-day implementation.

Born in the Netherlands, Mark currently lives in Venice, California, and is an independent entrepreneur and marketing consultant. Previous to his move to the Los Angeles area, he was senior advisor and marketing director with Brodeur Marketing Europe, a highly successful consultancy firm specializing in strategic marketing for companies in the ICT sector.

Before joining Brodeur Marketing in June 2001, Mark was Vice President of Marketing at RING! – a software company creating voice processing software for Telecom companies and call centers.

Mark introduced Telecom services for Castel (now called Essent Kabelcom), one of the largest cable companies in the Netherlands.

From 1986 to 1995 Mark was product marketing manager for WANG (three years) and Apple (six years).

Mark started his career in 1981 as software architect and trainer with his own company I.A.P.

Preface

It was in 1985, when I was working as a trainer at WANG Computers in the Netherlands, that I decided that product marketing was my next career change. The 'digital revolution' was going on and I felt eager to participate. Micro-computers were evolutionary from a technological point of view, but they were revolutionary from a user's point of view. The display of a personal computer was with its 24 lines × 80 characters per line still closely related to the paper punched cards, which also had a matrix of 24 × 80. But putting a computer on a desk, in the hands of an 'end-user' created a revolution in the way computers were used and the way computers were perceived. As a trainer at WANG's training center, I often talked to the marketing people and to the engineers at WANG and I started to realize that a successful product is not the same as good technology.

It fascinated me back in 1985 to see what products were accepted by 'the market' and why other, clearly superior products (from a technological point of view) sometimes were rejected and never became successful. The real breakthrough and market acceptance is often related to a small detail that makes a product 'usable'. While the art of printing was invented in or around 1455 by Johann Gutenberg, it did not result in widespread acceptance of printed books. It was only after Aldus Manutius had the vision in the early sixteenth century that books should be small enough to fit in a human's hand (and in a saddle bag) and should for readability purposes no longer use the gothic fonts, that books were accepted by a large group of people.

It still fascinates me. And product marketing fascinates me, for it is the product manager that holds all ingredients to make technology usable, in other words: to create a successful product.

About the templates and processes shown in this book

In many places in this book I have given examples of calculations, forms, databases and processes. These are all available on my website: www.markbutje.com. Feel free to download them.

Mark Butje

Acknowledgements

This book could not have been written without the excellent support and assistance from my family, friends and colleagues.

To Hillary, my dear wife, thank you for your inspiration, for your unblinking editorial eye, relentless second-guessing and many suggestions. I am grateful for your patience and understanding.

To Wim Vrijmoeth and Tim de Boer of Brodeur Marketing, thank you for your honest feedback and the many hours spent discussing this book.

To John Jansen and IJme Schilstra of Pallas Athena, for your support, enthusiasm and allowing me to incorporate Protos – a wonderful tool and invaluable contribution to this book.

I would also like to thank my sons Tim, Daan and Bas.

CHAPTER 1

Product marketing for technology companies

Why product marketing is the most key position in any technology company

Objectives

This chapter sets the stage and the framework for the rest of the book. It describes:

1 The essence of product marketing.

2 Introduction to the product life cycle.

3 The product life cycle seen as a process.

4 The compound product life cycle.

5 Why a technology company is different from companies in other industries.

Marketing: Getting and keeping the right customers

Most people in business have an understanding of what marketing is all about – getting and keeping the right customers. Although you will find many definitions on marketing when you search for it, I like this definition best for its simplicity and usability. Marketing can be direct marketing, viral marketing, branding, customer relationship management, promotion and advertising, public relations and so forth. Product marketing is marketing that is focused on the product (or service) the company is bringing to market.

Product managers can be found in all kinds of companies, from pharmaceutical makers to furniture manufacturers and from fast-food chains to computer vendors. Regardless of the industry, product managers have one thing in common; they are responsible for the marketing of their product.

The responsibilities of the product manager vary from sector to sector and company to company – but all products have a life cycle. Understanding how to manage that product life cycle through each stage determines the success or failure of a product.

Descriptions of the product life cycle can be found in many marketing books and is graphically represented in Figure 1.1. After the introduction of a product, sales will first slowly pick up, before entering the growth phase of the product life cycle. Popularity increases, market share increases, and also competition will increase. The growth of sales will diminish and sales

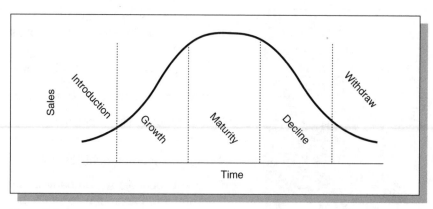

Figure 1.1 The product life cycle

will flatten during the maturity phase. With the introduction of competitive products and/or more competitors, the decline in sales is inevitable; and finally the product will become obsolete and will be withdrawn from the market.

The higher the amplitude and the broader the curve, the more successful the product is. The first line of this chapter stated that marketing is about *getting* and *keeping* the right customers. Getting the right customers will result in high sales and keeping the right customers will postpone the decline phase. Product marketing is all about optimizing sales results, in other words, optimizing the product life cycle.

Optimizing and controlling the product life cycle is easier said than done and starts way before the introduction of the product. It requires careful strategizing, planning, execution and control. Above all, it requires a process and methodology for all phases of the process.

The product life cycle process

Figure 1.2 is a high-level representation of the product life cycle process.

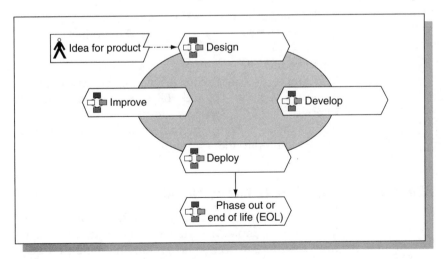

Figure 1.2 The product life cycle process

The stages of the product life cycle process are:

- *Idea*: This is the trigger of the process.

- *Design*: The attempt to get the right customers starts with a careful and methodical design and product definition, which includes a lot more than just the technical design.

- *Development of the product*: The realization, testing and, where needed, improvements of the design.

- *Deployment*: The deployment starts with the introduction of the product and starts the real product life cycle. Careful monitoring and continuous adjustments are needed in order to get and keep the right customers. We can recognize three sub-categories in the deployment phase:
  1 Production
  2 Selling
  3 Maintenance.

- *Improvement*: To extend the product life or increase the profitability, regular improvements to the design of the product will be needed. Reasons for improvements can have its origin in either one of the above-mentioned sub-categories. After describing the improvement needed, the process goes back into the design phase.

- *Phase out or end of life (EOL)*: At some point, it is no longer possible or wise to extend the product life.

This product life cycle is valid for any type of product. This process is also true for technology companies, those operating in the IT and Telecom sectors, generally referred to as IT companies. But the market characteristics for the IT industry are unique and so is the methodology required to make a product successful.

The product life cycle is like a fractal

Although the product life cycle as drawn in Figure 1.1 looks quite simple, it is actually the resultant of multiple product life cycles and at the same time a part of a bigger product life cycle. The product life cycle and its process are applicable to the technology, a product family, a product, a product version and so on. No matter how much you zoom in on it or out of it, it always behaves as a product life cycle again. In that way, it acts like fractal.

Example: The facsimile, better known as fax machine, was invented already in 1843 by a Scottish mechanic Alexander Bain. It was a very rudimentary machine consisting of a metallic contact resting on a moving paper slip saturated with an electrolytic solution. In 1865 the first working trials for a commercially viable fax machine was set up in France by an Italian, Caselli. Despite many improvements to the machine, such as the use of a photo-electric cell in 1902 and the use of coupling devices for the telephony network (PSTN) around 1930, the fax remained a cumbersome, expensive and difficult-to-operate machine.

In terms of product life cycle, the 'growth' phase only started after the Group 1 standard was agreed by the International Telegraph and Telephone Consultative Committee (CCITT) in 1968, followed by Group 2, Group 3 and Group 4 fax standards. Between 1973 and 1983, the number of fax machines in the United States increased from 30 000 to 300 000. By 1989 the number had jumped to four million and the compact fax machines available in the late 1980s revolutionized everyday communications around the world. So, before the fax really took off and became popular, both improvements to the technology itself as a multitude of products came and went. After the growth phase in the 1980s, products and technology did not stop improving themselves: from thermo-paper to plain paper; improvements in speed and ease-of-use; integration with printers and copiers; and so on and so forth.

By now, the trend is to move away from the fax. Email took a predominant role in communications and the combination of scanning, emailing and printing makes the fax machine in many situations redundant. Many subsequent technologies and products kept the fax at a high level of sales, but the fax seems to have reached the phase of decline in its product life cycle (Figure 1.3).

Fax technology itself is part of a bigger product life cycle. Call it 2D image transfer or (even bigger) communications technology, which is still just in its early maturity.

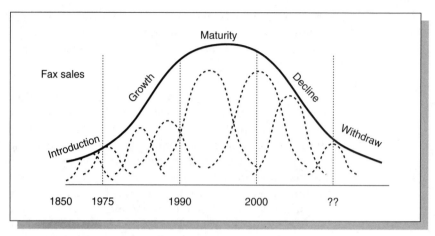

Figure 1.3 The compound product life cycle

What makes the IT company different?

The market changes extremely fast

The information and communication technology (ICT) market changes faster than any other market sector. Although Nike would like you to believe otherwise, a shoe is a shoe and the idea for a new design and its product life cycle is, for the most part, based on fashion, not technology. The short product life cycles of Nike shoes and other fashionable products are created artificially. Products in the ICT industry are based on technology advances – fashion is secondary. And the pace at which new products are cranked out and then become out of date by newer technology is faster than in any other industry.

In 1965, just four years after the discovery of the integrated circuit (IC), Dr Gordon E. Moore observed an exponential growth in the density of transistors in ICs, while costs per component were falling rapidly. Moore predicted that this trend would continue. The Press called it *Moore's Law*. For almost 40 years now, the famous Moore's law is still valid: 'The amount of components storable on a given amount of silicon has roughly doubled every 18 months since the technology was invented, and will continue to do so.'

The implication of Moore's law is that every year and a half the processor power doubles at the same or lower cost.

This is why new technology products are coming out at such a rapid pace. For example, with the introduction of a new computer, the vendor will have its successor already in development and the design for a replacement computer underway.

Moore's law can be applied to disk space, storage density, memory, transmission speed or other technologies.

Another, more general law says: 'Data expands to fill the space available for storage' (Parkinson's Law of Data). Or, whatever capacity is available will be used. This also applies to our daily lives. Look at your briefcase: No matter how big it is, it will always be full. The same is true for computer capacity. When DOS, the operating system for the 8088 personal computer (PC), was introduced by IBM in August 1981, it had a maximum addressable memory of 640 KB. At that time, no one imagined application taking up that much memory. Today, 256 MB of memory is the minimum of RAM needed to run a modern operating system on a PC. This increase beats Moore's law by five years. And the same rapid developments are true for other technologies. When we look at that first PC with DOS, we see a computer system with no hard drive and two floppy disks of 360 KB each. The first IBM PC (the XT) with a hard disk was introduced in March 1983. It had 10 MB of storage capacity. As hard disk storage also doubled every 18 months, 80 GB drives were available in 2003.

Higher capacity, better performance and new technologies are ever creating new opportunities for software developers. Software developers are always pushing the limits of computer capability, urging computer makers to increase performance, thus creating a vicious circle. The consequences of these short product life cycles are obvious. With the constant renewal of technology, the IT market is everchanging. The real innovators in the IT sector are often just slightly ahead of the early adaptors and majority.

This fast moving market is just one of the many fascinating aspects of product management in IT sector. It also presents many challenges. The product manager must juggle with upcoming and current products and is forced to think ahead in a market that renews itself every one and a half years.

Vendors in the IT sector tend to be technology-driven, not solution-oriented

Because of the rapid development of technology, with IT companies, there is of course a strong focus on the technology itself. But technology should not be the goal. Just a small part of the market buys technology for technology's sake. Most of us buy solutions made possible by that technology. What matters is how technology is applied to solve a certain problem or need.

With strong focus on technology and the necessity for ICT companies to continually renew their products and develop new solutions based on new technologies, they often forget why they are doing it in the first place. The goal should be to create new market opportunities, offer additional benefits and make a more attractive solution than the competition.

The developers or the 'techies' are a different breed than the commercial people, the sales guys. They think differently, they talk differently, they even look different. Most importantly, their motivation is different. More often, than in any other industry, there is a wide gap between the ones that develop the products and the sales guys. It is up to the product manager to build a bridge between these two worlds.

In the IT sector, the developers are the heroes and they should be. Their mighty brains create miraculous products and their creativity has changed our daily lives. From the way we communicate, transfer money or do business to entertainment and healthcare, technology rules us. But the heroes are always light years ahead of us. And while it is perfectly understandable that the heroes want to focus on technological innovation, in the end that is not what sells a product. Selling products is about benefits, functionality and what it does for the customer. Ultimately, it is up to the product manager to translate technology advantages into real solutions for the customer.

In the mid-1990s, telecom companies were showing off glass-fiber cables to attract new customers. One Dutch company even made paperweights from the cable and proudly handed it out to customers. Fiber optics was interesting for techies, but without explaining the benefits of this new technology, this was a totally useless sales argument.

Around the same time, increased processor power and the application of Digital Signal Processors (DSPs) made it possible to create telephone switches based on PCs (computer telephony). At the Voice + London Telecommunications Fair in 1997, I asked a sales representative for more information on a couple of telephone sets connected to a PC. He gave me a telephone handset and announced with great enthusiasm: 'Listen, a dial-tone. Can you hear it? And when you press the "1" button, it connects you to the set over there!' Although I admired his enthusiasm, this is more or less what you expect from a phone, don't you? I have to admit that using a PC for switching was new at the time, but without an explanation of what new possibilities, features and benefits came with this new technology, his demonstration was a complete waste of time.

The market buying behavior is different

The IT market shows an essentially conservative behavior

There is a strange paradox noticeable in the market for IT products. While the IT industry is cranking out this continuous stream of new and innovative products, the market shows an essentially conservative behavior. The market welcomes and asks for new solutions, but very few want to be the first to try them out. The market shows the behavior of a herd. It is hard to reach a level of acceptance, but as soon this level is reached the masses will follow almost immediately.

There are a couple of reasons for this reluctance to be the first to accept new products or new technology. First of all, it is important to realize that IT-based solutions can rarely be seen as isolated products. They are often just a small part of a complex environment. Changing one element in that environment might jeopardize the stability. In most companies these days, IT has become a key element in the business processes and the IT manager sticks to the principle that the IT environment should not be touched as long as it works. The stability of the system is the key responsibility of the IT manager, making him very conservative. IT products in the consumer market cannot be seen as isolated products either. The interchangeability of data, compatibility and the connectivity with peripherals and other systems or softwares should not be disturbed, unless it brings proven benefits.

A second important reason for the reluctance in the market to be the first to buy new products is the bad track record of the reliability of IT products. Flawless software does not exist, hardware often comes with all kinds of incompatibility issues. The 'time-to-market' pressure, the attempt to be ahead of the competition often results in the release of products which are barely tested. And when a new product hits the market, the first users of the product have to do without reliable product support. They are punished for being the first.

And then there is often the 'chicken-and-egg' problem with new technology. CD-ROM readers were introduced in computers back in the early 1990s, but there were almost no CD-ROM titles to make them attractive, so why buy them? And because no one had CD-ROMs built in their computer systems, software publishers did not see the benefit of using CD-ROM as a mass medium. In telecommunications, Universal Mobile Telecommunications Systems (UMTS) is a very promising technology that combines mobile phones and mobile data communication, but is useless without the proper infrastructure and the services that makes use of the new possibilities. But companies will only invest in creating the new services if and when there are enough owners of UMTS devices.

The IT industry is still experiencing growing pains

Although ICT products have changed the world and have had a profound effect on our daily lives, the technology industry is still relatively young. New products and technologies are tested in the market itself, without being based on customer demands or market study. The ICT industry has created its own language and imposed it on the market. The computer industry continues to praise their newest products in terms of clock-speed and video co-processors, forcing the poor buyer, who simply wants a new computer, to study complex features such as IEEE 1394, 802.11b and IDE-2.

But there are clearly signs that the market no longer just buys anything that comes out. People are comparing benefits and they demand solutions. The product manager of an ICT company has the difficult task of changing the company's focus from technology-driven to market-driven. In other words, they must help the company listen to the market and grow to maturity phase.

Conclusions

1 Product managers are responsible for the marketing of their product, in other words, for getting and keeping the right customers for their product.

2 Managing the success of a product requires understanding of the product life cycle and understanding how to manage the product life cycle. Strategizing, planning, execution and control require a process (the product life cycle process) and a methodology.

3 The product life cycle is the resultant of multiple product life cycles and at the same time a part of a bigger product life cycle.

4 The industry of IT and Telecommunication is different because:
   (a) The market changes extremely fast.
   (b) Companies in the IT sector are under pressure to continually bring out new products and technology.
   (c) Vendors in the IT sector tend to be technology-driven, not solution-oriented.
   (d) The market asks for solutions instead of technology.
   (e) The market buying behavior is different.
   (f) The IT industry is still experiencing growing pains.

5 All the conclusions above lead to the main conclusion: product marketing is a key position in any technology company.

So is the product manager super human?

Product Marketing for a technology company is one of the most challenging and exciting jobs out there. So does this person need to leap tall buildings in a single bound? No, of course not. Product Marketing is not magic, it is a profession that can be taught.

This book reveals proven methodology, including examples and practical templates, with the product life cycle process as the guide for the product manager.

Interesting links on the web

About the product life cycle

http://www.marketingteacher.com/Lessons/lesson_plc.htm
http://www.tutor2u.net/business/marketing/products_lifecycle.asp
http://www.fact-index.com/p/pr/product_life_cycle_management.html

On Moore's law

http://www.intel.com/research/silicon/mooreslaw.htm
http://www.thocp.net/biographies/papers/moores_law.htm

The spider in the web

Management by motivation

This chapter will discuss the roles and responsibilities of the product manager and the position of product marketing in the organization.

The questions this chapter will answer are:

1 What is the main responsibility of the product manager?

2 What ties to other parts of the organization does the product manager have?

3 What power does the product manager have to get the job done and achieve all the goals?

4 What are the *ten golden rules* for a successful product manager?

The product manager should be held margin responsible

The high-level role of the product manager is to make the product(s) successful. The previous chapter defined marketing as getting and keeping the right customers. The definition of 'successful' or 'the right customer' will vary from company to company. If the company goal is to be 'the biggest' or the company strategy prescribes to go for volume, then the success of the product and of the product manager will most likely be expressed in terms of market share. In some occasions, customer satisfaction will be the Key Performance Indicator (KPI), or the Quality of Service (QoS). The financial performance is important for every company, whatever the (financial) goals are. No one else in the company than the product manager has the ability and overview to be able to balance the cost of a product with the quality and functionality, the sales efforts with the gross margin per product. Everything the product manager undertakes and decides has an immediate effect on the contribution of the product to the performance of the company. That is why, whatever other parameters, the product manager will be held responsible for or is measured against, above all the product manager should be held *margin responsible* either as a percentage of the product revenue, the absolute value or a combination of both.

In order to be able to make the product successful, the product manager has to deal with virtually each and every department of the organization.

Imagine each department in your organization linked together to form a giant web, than you as the product manager are right in the center of it – like a spider (Figure 2.1).

First of all there is, of course, the market itself. In order to make the right decisions, the product manager needs to know the market thoroughly. This requires continuous attention and study. Without extensive knowledge on pricing, trends, technological developments, competition, market volumes, segmentation, channels and market influencers, the product manager is simply ill-equipped to do the job.

As the product manager, you act as a go-between for the technical and the commercial departments, translating technology into user-benefits and Unique Selling Points (USPs). Developers and salespeople are two very different type of persons and you are the bridge between them.

Then there is a third species, the finance manager. The ICT market is full of risks and every new product

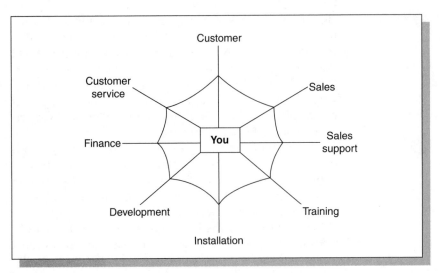

Figure 2.1 The spider in the web

requires new investment in development, promotion, sales, distribution and product support. A good finance manager guards the company's money like a dragon guarding its treasure. At the same time, the product manager is held margin responsible for the product. The financial director will almost always ask for more guarantees than the product manager can give. Chapters 8 and 9 focus on the many financial aspects of product marketing, including cost price calculations, calculations for Return on Investment (ROI), Break Even Point (BEP) analysis and pricing strategies.

But a product is not just a set of features with a price tag attached to it. A product is surrounded by services, support and the right distribution channel. Training must be developed not only for customers but also for sales, customer service and other departments and should be fully in line with the positioning of the product. It is up to the product manager to assure that all of these things are in place.

Promotion is also important. The product manager must work closely with Marketing Communications people to ensure that right message is sent out and Public Relations to arrange the right press attention and speaking opportunities.

But the product manager's job does not end with the developers and the commercial departments. Production should be in synch with expected sales volumes and the forecast should not exceed the maximum amount that can be produced. Nothing is more killing for a product than a flashy introduction and a failure to deliver. Remember, the life span of a product in the ICT sector is very short. And although the product manager is not responsible for the actual production, plans and expectations should be kept realistic.

Distribution is another essential link. Keeping products in stock costs money, but having no stock has an obvious impact on delivery time. The distribution department relies heavily on the product manager for information on how, when and how much to ship.

In order to reach the intended target market, the right sales channels must be chosen and developed. In most organizations, indirect sales, such as resellers, is the responsibility of the sales department. But managing a reseller is one thing – steering them in the right direction from a marketing point of view is another. The dealer channel needs its own positioning and good reasons to sell your product.

It is up to the product manager to bring all of these internal and external factors together and point them in the right direction. Acting as a 'spider in the web', a product manager can truly make or break a product.

The powerless CEO

The product manager is a weird person – someone who takes on an enormous amount of responsibility without actually being in charge. Sort of like a CEO without the hierarchic power. But it is important to point out that the product manager is not actually responsible for all of the departments that he or she is dealing with. They must instead guide everyone in a direction that is ideal for the product.

The biggest puzzle is that the product manager is responsible for the success of a product (and will most likely have a part of their salary attached to that success). All of this depends on the willingness of others to cooperate, while none of the key players in the product life cycle process reports to the product manager. The power the product manager does have is the power to inspire, convince and motivate the others around him and come to agreements with them on what they will deliver.

What the product manager *is* accountable for is the information handed over to the rest of the company; information that allows others to best do their job. Information in the form of guidance, directions and expectations. Information about budgets available, timelines, rules and conditions.

The product manager is the CEO of their own product – but a CEO without the power.

Methodology and attitude

How do you get things done without the power to order people around? It comes down to a thorough methodology combined with the right attitude. The methodology is described in the chapters to follow. Attitude is explained in the following rules.

Ten golden rules of product marketing

1 *Focus, focus, focus; carefully position your product – do not shoot on everything that moves*: The most frequently made mistake is trying to be everything for everybody. Do not try to tell the world that your product solves the problem for any person and any company. Even if it could – do not say it! Do not go after every opportunity that pops up. Make your choice and stick to it. Carefully position your product and make people think 'Hey, they are talking to me! That thingy is created especially for me.'

If you shoot on everything that moves, it is unlikely you will catch anything.

2 *Sell the solution, not just the technology*: You will find the above stated over and over again in this book, for it is an essential part of your role. The technicians in your company will not do this for you. They live for technology. And sales people cannot be expected to be able to figure this out for themselves. Technology is just an enabler for the solution.

But I would like to take this one step further. Try to hide the technology as much as possible. The more complex the technology, the more it should be hidden under an easy-to-understand interface. If you pick up the phone to call someone, you do not need to know how the connection with the other party is set up or the fact that the transport of your voice is going through copper, fiber or wireless connections. The same can be said for the first consumer video cameras which were not successful because it was too much of a hassle to set the right shutter speed and adjust the white-balance. These devices only became very popular after all of this technology was hidden behind a red button that did it all.

3 *Communicate and share the information you have – do not sit on it*: You as the product manager have an enormous amount of information at your disposal. Share this with the rest of the company. Keeping it to yourself might give you a feeling of power, but when you do not share, it almost always fires back on you. Without information, the people around you will start guessing. They are guessing about what will be in the next release and when it will arrive. And they will eventually begin to guess about what you are doing all day.

Sharing your information gets everybody on the same track and it allows others to come forward with good suggestions and feedback. By giving information, you will more easily receive information from others. So do not sit on it, but let it work for you.

4 *Take an active approach towards product development – do not wait for development to come up with yet another piece of technology*: Developers are very creative people. But, if you do not stimulate them to create the technology needed for your products, they will define their own challenges. Your attitude toward the developers should be an active and stimulating one. Be in touch, show your interest and visit their labs on a regular, and not necessarily scheduled, basis.

The first handwriting recognition software recognized approximately 80 percent of all words written. This was a very impressive breakthrough from a technology point of view, but unusable in almost any end-user product. So do not wait for development to come up with yet another piece of advanced technology. Advanced technology does not add up to market acceptance and a great solution.

5 *Actively bring sales into scoring position – do not be passive*: Giving sales all kinds of tools and brochures is

not good enough. Never just hand sales the product and the pricing and wish them good luck. That would be a far too passive approach. Ask them what you can do to help them score and bring them into position.

Always check to see if your efforts to help sales are having the desired effect and if not, adjust them. The more successful the sales team, the more successful you are and the more successful the whole company is. Consider yourself an important member of the sales team because you are.

6 *Look at your offering from the customer's perspective – do not look from the inside-out but from the outside-in*: The way you see the world is not nearly as important as how the world sees you and your product. With everything you do, try to step out for a while and look at what you are doing, from a customer's perspective. Imagine yourself as a customer, using your product for the first time. Try to read your brochure as an outsider. Are you speaking their language?

If you are a supplier of hardware and the serial number is the first thing your customer service people ask for, do not put it in some unreachable place where the customer has to crawl around on his knees, moving furniture around in order to find the 15-digit number.

When giving a presentation, ask yourself; how important and captivating is my 20-minute company introduction?

As soon as you are able to look at your company and the product you are marketing from the outside-in, you will be able to reach the customers and gain their appreciation.

7 *Blame yourself when the product is not successful – do not blame others*: You are the spider in the web and you can influence other departments to do what is needed to make the product a success. You, and only you, are responsible for your product.

It is always very easy to blame the sales department when sales is slow. So, sales is not aggressive enough? Then *you* go over there and do a better job motivating them, and provide them with the right tools to be aggressive. Sales does not know what they are talking about? Well, *you* teach them! They are fully relying on *you* to be taught how to sell the product, what the USPs are and how to deal with the competition. Is sales trying

Read more about the positioning statement in Chapter 5

to sell the wrong features to the wrong prospect? Then take them by the hand and point out who the right prospect is. Make sure they can recite your positioning statement in their sleep. Is sales spending too much time on each prospect? *You* should look at the number and quality of the leads you have generated.

The same goes for developers. If they are not developing what you expect, then first have a good look at how you instructed them and how closely you are following their progress.

And maybe the design of your product was based on the wrong assumptions or perhaps market circumstances have changed. All this comes down to *you*. Your job is to make the product a success.

You are the only one in the whole company, who can oversee the whole offering and the whole product life cycle. Listen to the people around you – if they have a critique, there will most likely be useful information in it. Evaluate what is happening with your product and take the necessary measures. If the product is not successful, there is no one to blame but yourself.

8 *Result-oriented promotion – no checkbox marketing*: I do not think any marketing manager would deny that in the end, it is the results that count. And yet, I have seen many presentations that only show what has been done during a marketing campaign and the results are not included. 'We printed 50 000 brochures, participated in four major exhibitions and 100 prospects visited our road shows!' So what? What was the outcome? And what is the ROI of the marketing dollars spent?

I call that 'checkbox marketing'. Creating a website is not enough. So what if you have 50 000 hits on your website. You should be measuring the conversion rate. Only the effectiveness of your marketing efforts counts.

9 *No spreadsheet marketing*: A spreadsheet has magical powers. Show anybody an impressive spreadsheet full of numbers, and they will not question the outcome.

In the early 1980s, I knew an accountant who often went to meetings with an enormous stack of green-lined computer paper, filled with tables and numbers. He only had to look somewhere in his computer output to make his point unquestionable. It came out of the computer, so it must be true. Today we know better, but the spreadsheet seems to hold that same power.

The danger of a spreadsheet is that you can easily manipulate the parameters in order to achieve an outcome to your liking. But the parameters should be based on honest facts and defendable assumptions.

Do not fool yourself and the rest of the company by fumbling around with the parameters for the sake of a more desirable outcome, no matter how tempting it is.

10 *Sell what you have – no 'next release' marketing*: No product is as important as the product you can currently sell, even though probably 70 percent of your time and attention is focused on the new release currently in development. Only the product that is available now can bring in the dollars. So when communicating with your target market, you have to stay focused on the benefits that your current product offers.

As soon as you start talking about the next release and that it will have even nicer features, is twice as fast and will be available in five fashionable colors, your prospect will wait for that next release. Or the prospect will be less happy with the current version then he would have been without any knowledge of the next release. Do not market your next release until it is available.

Keep the golden rules in mind when applying the methodology.

Conclusions

1 The product manager is the bridge and interpreter between the developers and the salespeople.

2 It is advisable to hold the product manager margin responsible for the product(s).

3 In order to reach the goals set, the product manager has to deal with almost every department of the company, without hierarchical power.

4 The product manager has to use his/her power to inspire, convince and motivate others around him to come to the desired agreements.

5 The right attitude is as important as the right methodology.

The ideal product manager in a technology company is capable of motivating all parts of the organization in order to create the ideal product and circumstances to make the product successful.

Mostly the product manager has some degree in technology and great interest in the commercial side. Some product managers are commercially educated and have a good feeling for and interest in technology. Communication skills need to be excellent and the product manager can motivate and steer others with infectious enthusiasm. This allows the product manager to build the bridge between development and sales, translating features into benefits and technology into solutions.

Interesting links on the web

http://www.productmarketing.com/topics/02/01.htm

The product life cycle process

From idea to deployment and back

Objectives

In this chapter, we will have a closer look at the product life cycle process, zooming in to the different stages. Each stage can be seen and is described as a sub-process. This approach to the product life cycle process will provide you with a structured way of working, checklists and examples. The subjects in this chapter are:

1 How to assess an idea for the development of a new product?

2 Why the rest of the company should be involved at an early stage?

3 Why the product design needs to start with the development of a product strategy?

4 The process for strategy development.

5 How to develop your functional specifications from a user's perspective?

6 How to create a product plan?

7 Tips on how to get the approval of the management team for the development of the product.

8 A closer look at the development process: It is not just a matter for the engineering department alone.

9 How to control the performance of your product during the deployment stage?

10 How and when to make improvements to your product to extend its life?

Now that we have described the ideal product manager, one who acts as a spider in the web, dealing with the heroes of technology, the soldiers of sales and the watchdogs of finance, you may be disappointed to hear that they are nothing more than a mere mortal. Everyone makes mistakes. This chapter provides product managers with practical tools and tips including checklists and examples to help make life easier.

The methodology given in this book will closely follow the product life cycle process (Figure 1.2). Figure 3.1 is

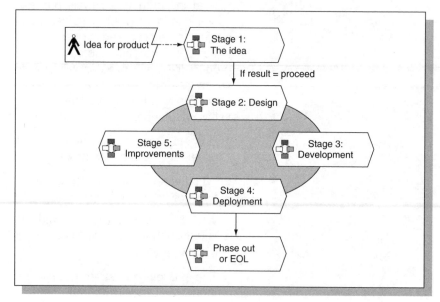

Figure 3.1 Top view of the product life cycle process

that same product life cycle process drawn again, but this time with one extra stage (or sub-process): the processing of an idea for a new product. Many ideas are born in technology companies, but no more than 15 percent of all ideas will make it into development. Of all products developed, only half will ever be profitable.

This is a high-level view of the product life cycle process. There are of course many more stages and all kinds of decisions to be made are not illustrated in Figure 3.1. But it is a start and fits the 'top-down' approach. In this chapter we will take an in-depth look at the different stages of the process and fill in the details to complete the process.

Each of the stages in the above process can be seen as a sub-process.

Stage 1: The idea for a new product

So someone in the company has an idea for a new product, perhaps triggered by some new technology or demand from the market. With any great idea, it is often tempting to immediately launch into development and surprise the rest of the company with some new product or a piece of technology. This is almost common practice, but not the wisest way to move forward. So you might argue that the best start for a new product is to do marketing research and write a business plan (which I call in this book the 'product plan') to prepare a go or no-go decision on the development of the product.

But assembling a product plan is a lengthy process, so before you even start creating one, try taking one step back. First share the idea with a cross section of people from the organization. Communication is key. Without communication there is no motivation for others to help turn this idea into a real product. In talking to others, you will benefit in multiple ways:

- Feasibility and attractiveness of the idea is determined at an early stage. The idea can then be taken to the next step, postponed or shelved altogether.

- By picking the brains of your colleagues you can obtain valuable information for product design.

- By simply pitching the idea you will have early buy-in from your colleagues. This type of support will be needed later on during product development and deployment stages.

From my experience, an attractiveness and feasibility study is best done during a brainstorm session. As the product manager, you act as the chairman and facilitator. This type of session should be well prepared and properly structured, and should take no more than two hours. If these hours are well spent, you will have saved yourself a lot of time, regardless of the outcome.

While preparing for an attractiveness and feasibility session, begin with the description of the idea. Anyone can come up with a brilliant idea, but not everyone knows how best to describe it. It is up to you to present the idea in an attractive way which forces the others in the session to focus on the benefits. For this purpose I have provided a questionnaire which should be completed by the originator of that idea (Figure 3.2).

Additional questions, such as these, can be added to the form:

- Would this product replace existing products or add to the company's portfolio?

- How would this product generate extra revenue?

- How much would this product sell for?

Whatever questions are added to the form, remember to keep it simple! Once the product idea has been clearly described, the brainstorm session can be organized. Schedule the meeting and send an advance copy of this completed description to those scheduled to attend.

Who should be included in the brainstorm session?

Invite representatives from departments that will in any-way be involved in the product.

- *Development*: Their contribution to the session is vital. They can give valuable feedback on the feasibility of the product-idea, point out previously unforeseen problems and come up with additional ideas, alternatives

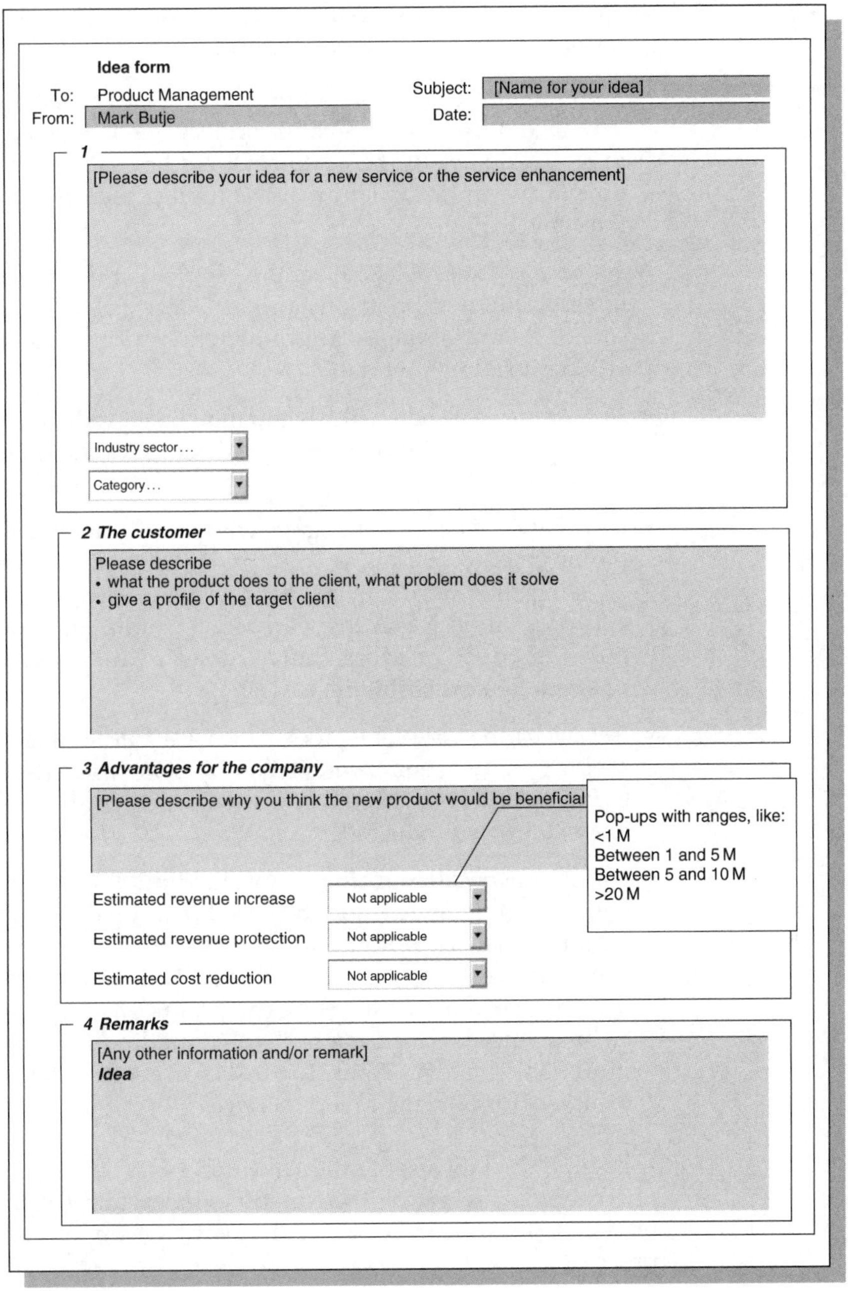

Idea form

To: Product Management

From: Mark Butje

Subject: [Name for your idea]

Date:

1

[Please describe your idea for a new service or the service enhancement]

Industry sector... ▼

Category... ▼

2 The customer

Please describe
- what the product does to the client, what problem does it solve
- give a profile of the target client

3 Advantages for the company

[Please describe why you think the new product would be beneficial

Estimated revenue increase — Not applicable ▼

Estimated revenue protection — Not applicable ▼

Estimated cost reduction — Not applicable ▼

Pop-ups with ranges, like:
<1 M
Between 1 and 5 M
Between 5 and 10 M
>20 M

4 Remarks

[Any other information and/or remark]
Idea

Figure 3.2 Example of an idea form

and even new opportunities. Developers can also give estimates on time and costs involved.

- *Sales*: A salesperson's first impression on the attractiveness of an idea should never be undervalued. After all, they are closest to the customers. Additionally, sales people add an important non-technical perspective to the conversation.

- *Service and Support*: These are the people that will have to service and support any product once it has been sold. If there are suggestions or objections to an idea, it is better to know up front.

- *Manufacturing*: They will have to make the product, so like Service and Support any feedback is valuable to the session.

- *Distribution*: These are the guys who know how to get the product to market. Is software distributed on CD or using the Internet and what are the consequences and possibilities? Can the warehouse handle the proposed product or what can be done in the design phase to make distribution easier?

- *Installation*: In case your product is not a 'shrink-wrap' product and it requires installation by your installation technicians, they too should be invited to give their opinion on the new-product-idea.

- *Finance (optional)*: Getting a product produced can have major financial implications for any company. Because financial officers do not easily part with the company's money, it is often a good idea to include them in the process early on. The product also needs to be invoiced, which might involve modifications to the billing system. Think for instance about a telco company introducing i-mode services.

A new product idea is not the same thing as a new piece of technology, so get all the experts together and solicit opinions. Pick their brains and involve them in the process.

The agenda

Create a very simple agenda, such as this one, with time for discussion.

1	Introduction	15 minutes
2	Positives	30 minutes
3	Objections	30 minutes
4	Suggestions	30 minutes
5	Conclusions	15 minutes

Ad 1   Clarification of the idea. This is best presented by either the product manager or the originator of the idea.

Ad 2   For the first half hour of the session, allow *only positive arguments*. You should be strict on this point. This saves time and helps the creative process. Any objections can wait until the second half of the session. Using a whiteboard or flipover, listing categories and subjects such as listed below can help with the flow of ideas:
(a) Company strategy fit
(b) Portfolio fit
(c) Revenue opportunities
(d) The advantages from a customer's perspective
(e) New markets/new customers
(f) Image and PR opportunities.

Ad 3   Allow each person to bring up concerns and issues that they believe that need to be addressed. Ask even the creator of the idea to come up with at least one disadvantage or concern.

This focusing on first the positive arguments only and then the negatives only is a method to stimulate the creativity and to stay out of polarizing discussions. The smartest idea will still have some issues or concerns and even the most unrealistic idea will have a positive element. That positive element can trigger great new ideas.

Ad 4   Spend the next 30 minutes trying to solve these issues and concerns. You have all the experts in one room and their combined brainpower should focus now on solving. What need to be done to eliminate the issues? Or, how can we make use of the advantages and opportunities that are listed in point two? At this stage of the discussion, the original idea may change dramatically.

Ad 5 At the end of the session, a decision should be made on whether to proceed. Remember, this is not yet a commitment to actually develop the product. If the choice is to go ahead with the idea, a more precise description of the product, market, positioning, pricing and other aspects will be developed at a later time. Store all of the information collected during the session in a 'product idea pool', even if the idea is rejected or postponed.

By this point you have already collected an enormous amount of valuable input, and should be well informed enough to begin writing a product plan. Most importantly, you have shared information with each department, and have therefore enlisted their cooperation from the beginning.

Figure 3.3 shows the steps in the processing of the idea for a new product.

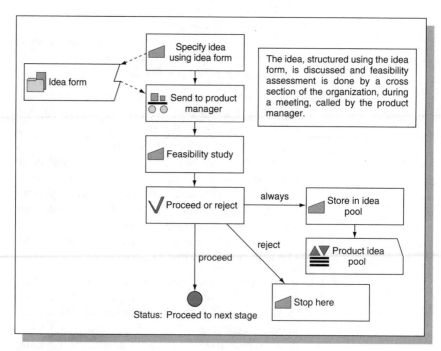

Figure 3.3 Stage 1 – the idea for a new product

Stage 2: Design

Traditionally, the design phase means coming up with functional and technical specifications for a new product. Resist the temptation to immediately begin writing a product definition and instead approach the design plan from a marketing perspective. The marketing perspective means that you first have to analyze the situation, research what options you have, make your choice that fits best with the company strategy and then create your product strategy.

Product strategy development

The development of marketing strategy for your product is analog to the strategy development of a company.

Figure 3.4 shows the methodology as a process flow.

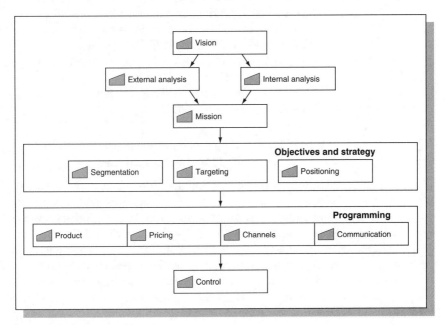

Figure 3.4 Strategy development process

Revisit your organization's vision and mission. How does this new product contribute to the realization of company's mission statement? How does it fit with the company's vision? Create similar statements for your new product:

Vision: A company's vision should clearly explain its 'reason for existence'. Additionally, this statement should express how the company looks at the future and what it aims to realize.

The vision related to a product or a new technology is not that much different and expresses the wider reason for the product. It helps in putting the product in perspective, both internally and externally.

Example: On its website for Bluetooth products, Philips puts the Bluetooth technology in perspective by formulating its vision:

> Global communications, instant accessibility, convergent applications – these are the major trends in the industry today and connectivity is the driving force behind them all. [. . .]Philips is an active member of the Bluetooth Special Interest Group (SIG) and Wireless Ethernet Compatability Alliance (WECA) for work with 802.11a and 802.11b. Philips understands that for true connectivity we must provide seamless solutions for WLAN, WPAN, WWAN always keeping end-user in mind.

Write down a same type of *raison d'être*, clearly spelling out why this product is being introduced.

Read Chapter 4 for an in-depth explanation on how to define your product mission

Mission: Just like a company has a mission statement, defining where the company is heading and what their long-, mid- and short-term goals are, a product should have a similar set of goals: The Product Mission. You have already described in your product vision what the reason is for the creation of the product, but now you also have to set yourself goals, the 'marching orders' explaining to everybody where you are heading with the product. In order to be able to do so, you first have to do some analysis, broaden your view, list the options and then come to realistic, yet ambitious, goals.

After describing the product vision, perform an *internal and external analysis*. This will help you determine your strategic options and explore the possibilities for your product. Chapter 4 describes these steps in detail.

Remember: If you do not set a goal, it is very unlikely that you will score!

Strategy: Now that you have set a goal for the product-to-be, you need to begin developing a strategy, which is divided into three elements:

1 Segmentation

2 Targeting

3 Positioning.

In Chapter 6, you will find a step-by-step guide about how to come to your product positioning, and methods on how to segment the market. This all is closely related to your product mission and needs to be done before you can create your product specifications. This top-down approach of designing the product makes the product development truly marketing-driven, as opposed to technology-driven. It will help you in prioritizing and making choices during the writing of the functional specifications.

Once this part of the design stage has been completed, you have already laid the groundwork for your product. You have analyzed your options by looking at internal and external factors, set goals and expectations, investigated possible market segments and identified target customers.

The functional specifications

It is now time to create the functional specifications of the new product. In order to reach that targeted customer, you should have a pretty good idea of what unique features the product offers. While the creation of functional product specifications is the responsibility of the product manager, close cooperation with developers is highly recommended.

A functional specification describes how a product will work, entirely from the user's perspective. That is why it is important that you first did your research and product positioning. You know your target customer.

Unfortunately, many (if not most) technology companies think they can skip the writing of the functional specifications. Especially software developers and programmers tend to think they can save time by immediately start writing code. It is the biggest mistake you can make and an unnecessary risk.

Here are some of the subjects that should be part of your functional specification:

- *Scenarios*: When you bear designing a product, you need to picture in your head and describe some real live scenarios for how people are going to use it. You know your product's audiences. Imagine a fictitious, stereotypical user from each audience who will use the product in a totally typical way. The more vivid and realistic the scenario, the better a job you will do designing the product for your real or imagined users.

- *Non-goals*: When you are building products with a team, everybody tends to have their favorite features that they cannot live without. But if you will do them all, it will take an infinite amount of time to realize the product and it will cost too much money. You have to set your limits and the best way of doing so is to include a section with non-goals. A non-goal might be a feature that is not needed ('no speech recognition interface') or it might limit the goals and expectations ('We can't care about performances in this release'). These non-goals are likely to cause some debate, but it is important to get it out as soon as possible.

- *Structure overview*: An overview of the structure gives the readers of your specs the big picture. It maps out the relation between different parts of the design. This can be a high-level flow chart or a drawing of the architecture.

- *Details*: Finally, go into the details. At this point, you will most likely need help from the developers, for they can provide you with feedback and lots of questions and comments to make sure you cover all areas needed. It is often handy to create a database in which you can store all your details, allowing for sorting, categorizing and easy retrieval. Information you should add to your description of the detail:
  - *Category*: such as user interface, function, compatibility, interface and so on.
  - *Part of*: to be able to group the functions in another way than on category. The 'part of' refers to the bigger picture or the architecture of the product.

- *Priority*: rank from 'must have' to 'nice to have'.
- *Picture (if applicable)*: Pictures are especially important to define the user interface. Fake screenshots of a software interface for instance are often far more descriptive than words can be.
- How and when the described detail will be used.

● *Open issues*: The first specification will certainly not be complete and it is OK to leave open issues. During the writing of the specs you will knowingly leave issues open. These can be flagged and if you also put them in your database, you can later in the process easily find them again.

The product plan

The product plan for a product is the equivalent to a business plan for a company

At this stage you should already know exactly what type of product you want to produce and why you want to introduce it. In the previous chapter you have read how the product manager acts like a CEO for his own product. And just like the CEO needs a business plan for the company, you have to create a business plan for your product, also known as the product plan. The purpose of the product plan is twofold:

1 To get approval from the board of directors to develop the product.

2 Provide everyone involved with a detailed guidebook to be used for both development and product launch.

Luckily, you have already written the first chapters of the product plan, created during the design stage. The additional chapters of your product plan, outlining financial implications, forecasts, timelines, initial launch ideas and departmental support needed, will give a complete picture of why your product should be developed and what will be done to turn it into a healthy business.

How to create the remaining chapters of your product plan is lined out in detail the Chapters 8, 9 and 10 of this book.

Appendix I provides detailed suggestions for the content of your product plan.

With finishing your product plan, you finished the design stage of your product.

Milestone: Go/no-go decision

This is a crucial moment for any product manager with a new idea. You must present your plans to the board of directors. Communication and presentation skills will be put to the test. But if you followed the steps above, you come very well prepared.

Let us say you have been given one hour to present all of your plans, conclusions and recommendations for this new product to the board. Be prepared that you will only have 15 minutes to tell your story, even if you are on the agenda for a full hour. As we all know, board meetings often run behind schedule. The goal is to deliver a short and powerful presentation even with time constraints.

Review your core message and be clear about what you expect from the board. Be careful not to oversell your ideas. Use your inspiration and enthusiasm to persuade them. Since you have already discussed many of these elements with people from other departments, give credit to those who offered suggestions and gave valuable feedback, this can help smooth the way.

Concentrate your core message around:

- The demand in the market.

- Explain how your product meets the needs of the market.

- Describe what this product will do for the organization, how it fits in with the company vision and mission. Also describe the product from the customer perspective.

- Talk briefly about planning and include a product launch date.

- Provide a spreadsheet with the financials, mentioning just the key indicators, such as investment funds needed, ROI, revenue forecast, margin and total contribution.

- Wrap up your presentation with a review of positioning statement and then ask for approval to proceed.

Remember, board members may not be as technically oriented as you are and may not know the market as well as you do. But they certainly know how to read the financial paragraph! Board members can offer product managers a hard time on issues such as forecasted revenue, investments needed and expected profitability. Make sure you have prepared a financial outlook with the help of someone from that department. This saves a lot of discussion.

Figure 3.5 shows the design stage as a process flow. In this process, the steps 'Strategy development' and 'Create Product Plan' are sub-processes themselves and are drawn in detail in Figure 3.4. And you are now ready for development.

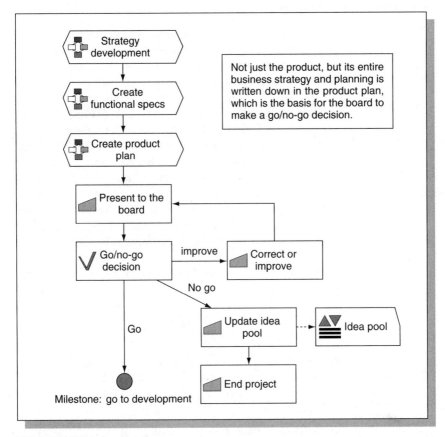

Figure 3.5 Stage 2 – design

Stage 3: Development

Let us say you have been given a 'go' from the board. This is an exciting time because after all of your hard work you can finally proceed with turning an idea into

Virtual product team: A group of representatives from all departments involved in the realization of your product

a real product. Expectations are high and it is up to you to make it happen. But there is no way you can do it alone. The time has come to really show off your talents as a motivator.

The development of a product is not just the responsibility of the engineering team. It requires the involvement of almost every department in the company. The formation of a Virtual Product Team helps to ensure that this product becomes a reality.

The kick-off meeting

Call a meeting with everyone involved to celebrate the fact that you, as a team, will create this great new product. Share and delegate responsibility and, however, you can try to create a bond between the members of that virtual team. Whether you hand out custom T-shirts or stage an after-work event to promote the Virtual Product Team, make people feel like they are part of something exciting.

Companies often assume that the creation of a new product is the sole domain of the engineers. But a new product in the ICT environment is not built by technology alone. It requires packaging, documentation, distribution, support, installation, marketing, sales, billing and collection. All of these departments should be involved from the beginning of the development process avoiding miscommunication and paving the way for success.

Here are some suggested items to discuss during the kick-off meeting:

- *The Product Plan*: Clearly outline all of the steps involved in the development of the product.

- *Responsibilities*: Make sure that each person in the room is given responsibility for at least one part of the project. That person will act as a liaison to their department.

- *The Project Plan*: Create a tool to track and report the progress of your project, even if it is simply an Excel spreadsheet. Require that all team members report their progress using that tool.

- *Reporting*: Schedule regular times for the Virtual Product Team to meet for progress reports and new developments.

- *Communication*: Develop a team communication strategy.

- *Create a group email address.*

- *Create a common storage space* for documents, project plans and updates and give the team exclusive access. If the team is scattered throughout different locations, create a special intranet site.

- *Develop a way to communicate* to the rest of the organization news about the product using new or existing channels such as a newsletter or website.

The development of the product

A market-ready product is the combination of the product itself + documentation, support, training and everything else to make it suitable for the end-user.

In this book, I am not zooming in on how developers translate functional specs into technical specs and how they actually develop the technology. That is in their expert hands and is beyond the responsibilities of the product manager. But development of the market-ready product is not the responsibility of the engineering team alone. While the developers are working on technique, the rest of the company can begin developing ways to support the product, such as marketing materials, billing and collection systems and, for example, a public relations strategy. You as the product manager are at the helm of this process.

The development of the marketing materials and the preparation of the product launch are described in more detail in Chapter 7, for this is your direct responsibility.

OK to release

Before a product can be released, each member of the Virtual Product Team should officially sign-off on the new product. This transition step, referred to as OK To Release (OTR), indicates to everyone that development is complete and everything is in place to move on to the next step: commercially launch the product.

OK to release can be compared to what happens during a pit stop at a Formula One race. A car comes to a stop and a crew in brightly colored overalls works at breakneck speed to change a wheel, pump gasoline or replace the front section of the car, sometimes in less than five seconds. As each crew member finishes, they raise a hand to confirm. The pit boss stands in front of the car until all hands are raised, only then is the car allowed back into the race.

I am sure the driver is grateful if the pit boss does not give way without a complete showing of hands . . .

The same thing is true for the release of a product. A showing of hands is not very practical, but an official sign-off serves the same purpose. As the product manager, you are the pit boss of this new product. The OTR serves as a final quality check and official sign-off for each member of the Virtual Product Team. This step also ensures that everyone involved is responsible for their actions and can take credit for the success or failure of the product. Once the OTR milestone has been met, your product is ready for the next phase.

The development of a product is drawn as a process in Figure 3.6.

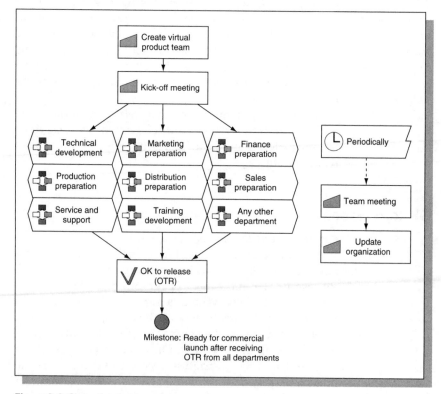

Figure 3.6 Stage 3 – development

Stage 4: Deployment

The race to successfully market the product has started and sales is in the driver's seat. As the product manager, you have done everything you can to prepare: setting goals, creating strategies and forecasting financial expectations. But like a Formula One race, even though the product has been launched, circumstances in the market or on the race track can still change. It is crucial that you continue to assess the market and the whole delivery process.

Let us say parameters in the market suddenly have changed. The competition has introduced a similar product, the economic climate has worsened or perhaps, the price does no longer 'conform' to the market. This calls for an immediate switch in tactics, a change in strategy or even modification to the design itself. Once the product is finally deployed, it is important to closely monitor its performance; continue to gather information about the target market, seek new opportunities, study the competition and stay in close contact with your sales people.

Refer to Chapter 10 to learn more about the relation with the sales force

Communication between a product manager and a sales force is very important to the success of a product. Chapter 10 is dedicated to this topic.

Hopefully your product finds relatively quick success in the market. Be aware that the competition will most likely take notice of that success and try to counter it with a new product or market strategy. Stay alert and never think that your product is untouchable. The only stable factor in the ICT market is change, so use your marketing skills to stay competitive.

Control

The last element of the Strategy Development Process (p. 31) is about control.

It is important to create for yourself a process in which you evaluate the success of your product and determine if your strategy and tactics are producing the desired result. Many market changes are gradual and can easily escape your attention, so build in time for evaluation on a regular basis.

- Look at the goals you have set and compare them with the results. Analyze overall sales, revenue, margin, contribution and market share.

- Evaluate the internal and external analyses made before introduction. Did anything change? Are there new opportunities? New threats? New opportunities for partnering? Is your defined target segment and target customer still valid or does the product need to be repositioned?

- How is your product being received by customers? Did your promotion have the desired effect? Are your core messages clear? Is the promotion sufficient to generate awareness and an adequate number of new leads?

- Analyze questions and requests for service received by the help desk or customer service organization. Are there indications that the product lacks features? Is the documentation provided with the product clear?

- Join sales on customer visits. Which features and benefits appeal most to customers and which the least?

With more new ideas and products in development, there is often no time to go back to a product that is already on the market, except when sales results have dropped. By then it is often too late. Do yourself a favor and *plan the evaluation in advance*. By planning the evaluation, you stay in control.

Do it at least twice a year! The process flow as shown in Figure 3.7 does not look too complex. But the monitoring takes constant attention. The launch of the products is drawn as a sub-process and will be discussed in more detail in Chapter 8.

Hopefully, your product will find success in the market and beat all expectations. But as with all ICT products, you will eventually have to remove it from the portfolio, maybe to be replaced by an updated or new version.

Stage 5: Improvements

In case the monitoring, as described in stage 4, asks for measures, you carefully have to think what type of measures or adjustments are needed. If, for instance, sales is slowing down or below expectations, your sales reps might request a price decrease. A price drop might indeed be necessary, but before doing so, you can consider adjusting your positioning, your promotion and your

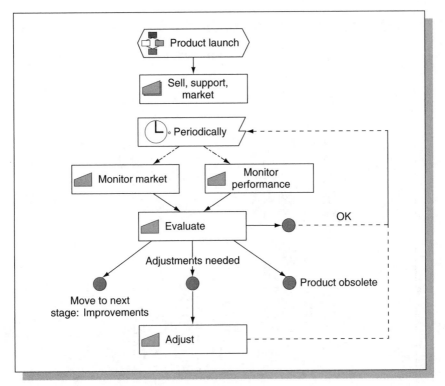

Figure 3.7 Stage 4 – deployment

target markets. Changing circumstances in the market can trigger the need for adjustments or improvements. In your evaluation, also have a critical look at the goals set – maybe they have to be revised as well.

Defining product design changes and improvements, such as features for a next release, is an ongoing process. The process of deciding what new features will go into the next release needs to be well coordinated with the development team. More about this cooperation with the engineers and hints for tools can be found in Chapter 11.

With the idea for a new or updated version of the product, the process starts all over again with the design stage.

The product life cycle process in detail

At the beginning of this chapter I showed you a simplified diagram of the product life cycle process. We have closely examined the different stages as sub-processes (Figure 3.8).

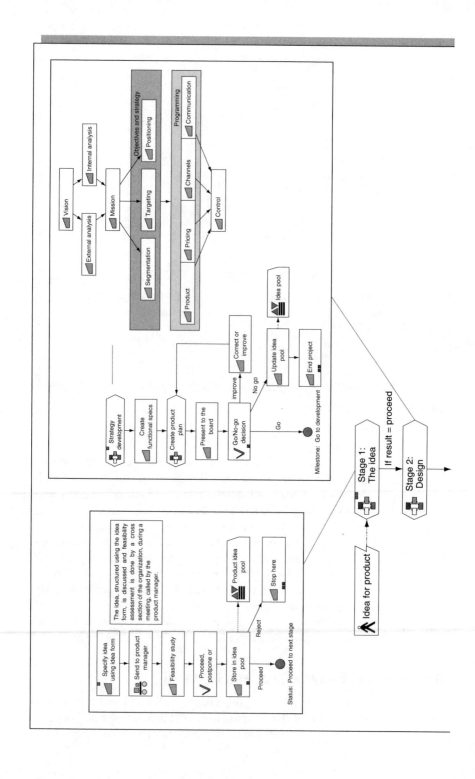

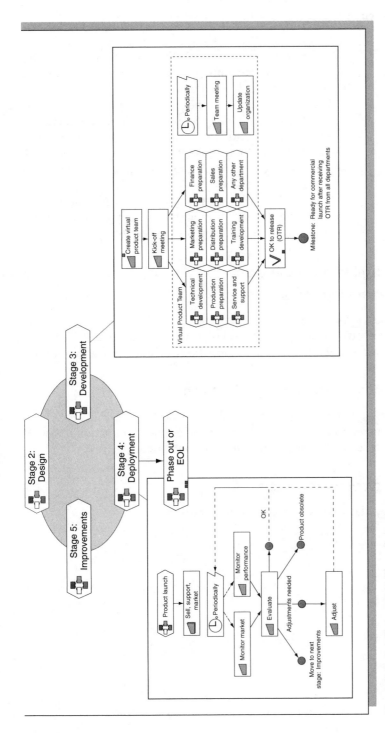

Figure 3.8 Detailed product life cycle process

Conclusions

Managing the product life cycle is a process. Like any other process, it starts with the definition of the goals and the results are compared with these goals, allowing for improvements and adjustments.

The responsibilities of the product manager are directly tied to the product life cycle process. From the moment a product idea is born to the end of its life, the product manager needs to work methodically and closely with key members of the organization to maximize the chances of that product's success.

By including all departments in the organization from the very start of the product life cycle, the product manager gets well-needed support and buy-in.

Interesting links on the web

About generating ideas

http://debonogroup.com
http://www.brunel.ac.uk/research/exploring/edp/Ideageneration.html
http://www.creativeadvantage.com/ideation_techniques_overview.html

About writing functional specifications

http://www.joelonsoftware.com/articles/fog0000000036.html
http://www.pragmaticsw.com/Pragmatic/Templates/FunctionalSpec.rtf
http://www.softwarereality.com/lifecycle/functionalspec.jsp

About improvement processes

http://www.uaa.alaska.edu/assessment/cip.cfm

Mission statement for your product

The man on the moon

Objectives

The objective of this chapter is to give you tools to set your goals for your product. The chapter will give you answers to the following questions:

1 What is a mission statement?

2 What is the importance of a mission statement to a product?

3 What is a SWOT analysis and how can it help to determine your options?

4 How to conduct internal and external analysis?

5 How to use a SWOT matrix to find your strategic options?

All companies have a mission statement, or at least they should have one. It helps organizations to stay focused and encourages employees to move in the right direction. A good mission statement also clearly explains to the rest of the world where the company is headed.

When President John F. Kennedy visited NASA in 1965 and asked a man, sweeping the floor with a broom, what he was doing, he answered: 'I am helping to put a man on the moon'. They had a powerful mission, and it was clear in everybody's mind what that mission was.

Every new product should also have its own mission statement. As opposed to the company mission statement, the mission statement for your product is not a statement you want to publish. It is the starting point for your product strategy and clearly defines to everyone in the company what the expectations are.

The product mission statement:

- is for internal usage

- sets the expectations and directions

- defines the purpose of the product

- contains the medium- and long-term goals

- helps to focus

- is the starting point for the product strategy.

When developing a mission statement one of the most obvious questions to ask is: What do we want to accomplish with this product and why? Is the product being created for a new market segment? Is the product a stepping stone for other types of product development? Is the product meant to be a prime revenue generator or is the goal to support other products? In order to clarify these goals, you need options and strategies to choose from. The product mission statement should also explain how it adds value to the company in terms of the realization of the company mission statement.

To be able to set the goals, you first have to broaden your view and analyze the situation, to find out what options you have. You most likely already have your opinion ready about the possibilities and the goals for your product. But try to put your bias aside and do your analysis with an open mind.

SWOT analysis = The analysis of the Strengths, Weaknesses, Opportunities and Threats

The proven method for determining what options you have for your strategy, is the SWOT analysis, the analysis of your Strengths and Weaknesses (internal) and the Opportunities and Threats (external) you see around you. Before you are able to analyze your strengths, weaknesses, opportunities and threats, you of course have to list them. Just listing them is often mistaken for the analysis itself, but it is just the starting point! Drawn as a process-flow in Figure 4.1.

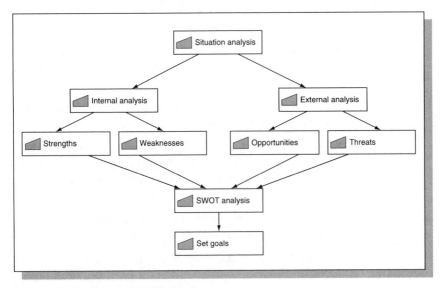

Figure 4.1 Situation and SWOT analysis

Listing your SWOT can best be done in a brainstorm session with a group of four to eight colleagues.

Internal analysis

Strengths and weaknesses

Take a look at your own company, examine the product or the product idea and then make a list of why your company or product is better than others. If you list company strengths, they need to be relevant to your product. The strengths must be those things that give you an advantage over your competitors. For example, if you have a team of developers with a lot of expertise on wireless networks, it might be tempting to list that as a company strength. But this is only relevant if your competitors have less or no expertise in this area. On the other hand, if you have a personnel shortage, but your shortage is by far not as bad as that of your competitors, that is a strength.

Be specific when listing company strengths. So if you think you have a strong dealer channel, explain why you think your dealer channel is strong. And if the company has an advantage in distribution, specify what that advantage is.

Topics that you might consider when specifying company and product strengths:

- *Specific expertise*: In what area has your company or people working at your company have exceptional expertise or special skills?

- *Market position*: Is there a market where you dominate or have a very strong position?

- *Geographic spread or location*: Being located close to airport, surrounded by other high-tech companies, in the heart of the financial district or other special locations can be real strengths.

- *Investors and financial position*: Is your financial position better than the position of your competitors?

- *Product mix*: Is the mix of products offered by your company more complete than the portfolio of the competitors? Are there products in your company's product portfolio that can be supportive to the success of your product?

- *Technology partners*: Does any of your technology partners or the relation between them and your company give your product advantages compared to your competitors?

- *Distribution*: How is the distribution done for your product and what organization do you have in place. Is it different from the methods used by your competitors and if so, is it a strength?

- *Sales channels*: Is your sales force at any point better qualified for selling the products? Are they more experienced? What about your dealer – retail channel or other indirect sales channels? How are they geographically spread and what is their expertise, commitment and ability to sell your product?

- *Marketing*: Can you develop more marketing power than the competition? Are there other marketing strengths?

- *Customer service*: How does your customer service relate to that of your competitors? Can they work cheaper or are they more responsive?

- *Development (unique tools; capacity)*: Are the engineers in your company using unique tools that create certain strength? Is your company to develop faster and bring products faster to market? Is there unique expertise in the development team?

- *Own(ed) technology*: Do you use different technology and how is that better?

- *Pricing*: Is your product priced competitively or do you have a better pricing structure?

- *Company image*: What is your company known for in the market? What strength does that give you?

- *Awareness and market share*: Is your market share high? Or the awareness of your company in the market relatively high?

The list above is not meant to be complete. These are examples of what you have to take into consideration when making the internal analysis. In a brainstorm session with your colleagues, it helps the thinking process to concentrate on specific subjects, like listed above.

After going through company strengths make a list of weaknesses. Again, include only relative weaknesses, meaning weaknesses that are weaker than the competition. And remember, be specific! You can go over the same list again as used for the strengths.

Strangely enough, I have discovered that most people find it easier to list their weaknesses than strengths. When creating a product strategy, company and product strengths are always more important than weaknesses.

External analysis

Opportunities and threats

Conducting an in-depth analysis of the market sector your company is operating in provides you with valuable information on opportunities and threats in the market.

First try to step outside of your own company and look at the market you are operating in with an unbiased view. List the opportunities offered, trying not to immediately relate them to your company. The evaluation of the opportunities comes later.

Topics to think about:

- *Competition and competing products*: Often competition is seen as a threat only, but they offer opportunities too. What was once a threat can sometimes turn into an opportunity in the market. For example, the 2002 bankruptcy of KPN Qwest left many European customers without service, presenting a huge opportunity for other infrastructure providers in Europe. Or let us say an innovative competitor of yours begins advocating some new technology or concept. Once there is a certain level of acceptance, they have in fact created an opportunity for you and other companies to jump into the market.

- *Economic situation*: Economic factors affect the purchasing power of potential customers and the firm's cost of capital. The following are examples of factors in the macro economy: Whatever the economic situation is, you will always be able to discover opportunities based on it. Some of the economic factors you have to take into consideration are:
  - *Interest rates*: If the interest rates are low, it offers the opportunity of low-cost financing.
  - *Currency*: Does the currency exchange rate make it easy to export? Does the exchange rate defend your position in your home market?
  - *Economic growth*: Even a recession or slowing economy can provide opportunities. In a situation where companies are hesitant to buy, outsourcing gets more popular for instance.

- *Job market*: Is labor scarce? Is knowledge scarce? What are the trends in your market? What are the opportunities?

- *Regulations*: An increasing number of governments are passing laws that forbid the use of a hand-held mobile phone while driving. This creates opportunities for a range of new products including hand-free sets, roof antennas, Bluetooth applications and installation services.

- *Technological trends*: The Internet is perhaps the most obvious of technological developments that continues to create opportunities for all kinds of companies. One example is the use of email to easily send pictures to anyone you want. This has led to a boom in use of digital photo cameras.

- *Change in customer behavior*: Consumer needs and preferences are constantly changing. Think about these changes and think what opportunities they might offer.

- *Social trends*: Social trends have a substantial influence on buying decisions. Think about fashion; think about changes in what is socially accepted.

To uncover potential threats in the market, once again take an unbiased look at the environment your company is operating in and go through the list again. Search this time for things that might threaten your company or product position in the market.

The SWOT analysis

'Strategy formulation is the development of long range plans for the effective management of environmental threats and opportunities in the light of corporate strengths and weaknesses.'

Wheelen and Hunger

Now number all the items you have listed in the following way. Strength number one will be S1, the second strength listed as S2 and so on. Also number weaknesses, opportunities and threats in the same way. Enter the numbered items into a matrix with four quadrants as illustrated in Figure 4.2.

All the ingredients are now ready for analysis. By mapping your internal strengths and weaknesses with the opportunities and threats in a matrix you can define the options you have on which you can base your strategy. The four quadrants in the matrix will give you options for four different types of strategy:

1 *Options for growth strategy and strategic focus*: Combine your strengths with the opportunities in the market.

2 *Options for strategy for defending your strengths*: Combine strengths and threats in the market.

SWOT analysis matrix	O1, O2, O3, O4	T1, T2, T3, T4
S1 S2 S3 S4	**Strategic focus and growth strategies**	**Strategies for defending your strengths**
W1 W2 W3 W4	**Strategies for improvements**	**Strategies for risk control**

Figure 4.2 SWOT analysis matrix

3 *Options for strategy for areas to improve*: This strategy comes from combining opportunities and weaknesses.

4 *Options for strategy for risk control*: Combine threats in the market with weaknesses.

Once you have listed all strategic options, closely analyze each possibility and make sure you have not excluded anything. After close review, pick the strategies you feel are the best.

Case study 4.1

Symeko, a small Dutch software company, created a product called docstyler, to '... consistently uphold your company style in your documents – thus giving the best possible expression to your precious, carefully built corporate image'. The product was almost ready, but it was not clear what the best strategy was for the company and what goals should be set for the years to come.

To determine their strategic options, they analyzed their strengths, weaknesses, opportunities and threats:

Strengths

S1   The software is designed with internationalization in mind and the software is easy to localize and can be used in a multi-lingual environment.

S2 In contrast with most house-style management software, there is no need for programming, only for configuration.

S3 Automatic distribution of house-style related documents (such as templates) to all users in the customer's company.

S4 Developers are highly skilled and experienced in writing software for processing complex documents and databases.

S5 Developers and management of Symeko have a conservative approach that fits with large organizations.

Weaknesses

W1 No marketing and sales experience inside the company.

W2 No sales channels yet.

W3 Product limited to integration with MS-Office products.

W4 No references yet.

Opportunities

O1 Over 90 percent of all companies have problems in guarding their house-style.

O2 The problem mentioned in O1 is the biggest in large companies.

O3 IT managers are conservative – they are reluctant to install new applications.

O4 End-user demand – They want to be able to easily create professional-looking documents.

O5 Trend – The usage of electronic distribution of documents increases, due to email and the possibilities of the portable document format (pdf) of Adobe's Acrobat.

O6 Trend – The need for pre-printed paper is decreasing and will further decrease due to the increased quality of color printers.

O7 Large organizations invested a lot of money in their house-style.

Threats

T1 Most companies are not fully aware of the violations against their house-style.

T2 Amateur creation of own templates is often seen as fun.

T3 Structural changes to MS-Office.

T4 Microsoft can become a competitor.

The strategic options for docstyler were examined by mapping the strengths and weaknesses with the opportunities and threats:

SWOT analysis matrix	O1: More than 90% companies do need house-style management	O2: Especially large companies	O3: IT managers are conservative	O4: User wants professional documents	O5: Trend – electronic document distribution	O6: Color printers are getting better	O7: Large companies invested a lot in house-style
S1: International S2: No programming needed S3: Automatic template distribution S4: Experience with complex documents S5: Conservative approach	S1S2S4O1O2O3O7: Target large, multi-national organizations S2S1O1O4O5: Future development – low-end house-style management tool as ready-to-go end-user product.						
W1: No marketing and sales experience W2: No sales channels W3: Limited to MS-Office W4: No references	W2S2O7: Build partnership with design studios W1W2O5O6: Seek partnership with Adobe						

Only the strategic options for growth and improvement have been explored. Symeko's docstyler is a brand new product. Symeko does not have a market position that needs defending.

The strategic options as listed in the case study are not defined strategies, yet. They represent the options to choose from.

In your own analysis, pay special attention to the first quadrant, the options for your growth strategies. For outlining a goal or goals for your product, the strategy for growth is the crucial part of your product strategy. Take some time to think about what strategy or strategies will be best for your product and fits best with your company.

After you chose your strategy, you have to get more specific and attach real goals to it.

Now you are ready to formulate the product mission statement. State the following:

- The opportunity you see in the market that you are addressing with your product and your company and how it benefits from your strengths.

- A distant objective that inspires others in the company. It expresses the challenge and the ambition you have with the product.

- A relatively close goal that is worth pursuing. To come to your distant objective, you will need some 'stepping stones'. These are your short-term objectives.

- Immediate objectives that can be started on at once.

Example: To address the increasing demand for secure Internet payment services, we bring product, XXX to market. With our strong distribution channel, technology partners and unique verification system, we aim for a 35 percent share of all Internet payment transactions within three years from now. To reach this ambitious goal, we aim to assign two additional distribution partners in the Asia/Pacific region to double our revenue in that area in the coming year. Product XXX will be launched in Q2 of our fiscal year.

Conclusions

Creating a strategy for your product first requires a goal: your product mission statement. This product mission statement is the focal point for everyone in your organization involved with the product in some way.

Before setting your goal and formulating the product mission statement, a SWOT analysis gives you understanding of the possibilities, and the options for growth strategies in the market around you. The SWOT analysis is the combination of strengths and weaknesses from the internal analysis with the opportunities and threats from the external analysis.

Based on the strategic option or options you select, you set your product goals for the medium to long term, and then the short term and attach some immediate objectives.

Now that you have a mission for your product, you can define the strategy to accomplish that mission.

Interesting links on the web

About writing a mission statement

http://www.tgci.com/magazine/98fall/mission.asp
http://www.businessplans.org/Mission.html
http://www.bplans.com/dp/missionstatement.cfm

About SWOT analysis

http://www.quickmba.com/strategy/swot
http://www.businessballs.com/swotanalysisfreetemplate.htm
http://www-tradoc.monroe.army.mil/mwr/integrated_swot_analysis.htm

CHAPTER 5

Product positioning

Creating a unique space in the mind of the prospective customer

Objectives

In this chapter, you will learn the importance of product positioning and how it not only will be the fundamental for all your marketing activities, but how it also shapes your product and is an integral part of it.

The subjects in this chapter are:

1 The definition of positioning.

2 A seven-step methodology for the creation of your product positioning statement.

3 How to assess market attractiveness and select your target market segment(s).

There is a battle going on out there and the battle is for mind share. There is an explosion of information and products and an increasing number of ways for companies to communicate to prospective customers about a product.

Positioning is the attempt to control the public's perception of a product or service as it relates to competitive products.

Whether marketing a piece of merchandise, a service, a company or even a person, positioning is crucial to the success of any product. Positioning of that product is about how you get into the mind of the prospective customer. You must first get into a prospect's mind and then occupy that space.

Today, all of our minds are occupied with various types of positioning. BMW – *The ultimate driving machine*, Nokia – *Connecting People*, Philips – *Let's Make Things Better*. Each of these products invokes an image that is forever stored in our mind. These short messages are the most condensed form of positioning and called the pay-off of a positioning statement.

When positioning a product, you want the prospect to recognize that your product is created especially for them.

This chapter gives a step-by-step approach on how to develop positioning for your product. After you have finished all the steps, you will be able to create a positioning statement that makes perfectly clear who you are targeting with your product, what you have to offer to them and why they should choose your product instead of your competitor's. Here are the seven steps:

Step 1: The company and product ambition.

Step 2: The ideal client.

Step 3: A look at the 'whole product'.

Step 4: The unique selling points.

Step 5: Leading the analysts.

Step 6: Market segmentation and market attractiveness.

Step 7: The positioning statement.

Step 1: The company and product ambition

The product you are about to introduce needs a face, an image. An image that to a large extent, you can create yourself. But whatever image you decide on, it is important to understand that it has consequences in the market and consequences on how you market your product.

The image of your product will be one of the first things that your prospect will or will not feel attracted to.

As a consequence, it will also have an impact on the margin and the volume, on advertising and packaging, on your customer service and distribution. It is about setting the customer expectations.

Ask yourself the following questions: Who are we? How do we want to be perceived? How do we want our product to be seen? Finally, in which of these categories does my company fit and how does that effect the positioning of my product?

The knowledge leader   In the ICT world, this type of company is known for its technical expertise. The knowledge leader's expertise is often reflected in its high prices. The knowledge leader receives admiration and respect. Examples of companies claiming knowledge leadership: Ernst & Young, Schlumberger.

The market share leader   The biggest. This type of company goes for volume. To become a market share leader requires a wide sales channel and an aggressive market approach. Examples are Microsoft, Sony, General Motors, Nike. Going for volume requires large marketing budgets combined with modest margins. The big advantage is that you are known and therefore more often considered.

The service leader   The most responsive and the most committed to customer satisfaction. One major advantage is customer loyalty. But claiming to be a service leader also sets high expectations. In the battle between Hertz and Avis, Avis claims the position as the service leader, exploiting that they are not the biggest. Their pay-off is 'We try harder'. Many of the telecom companies try to claim leadership in service. Those who cannot deliver on that promise are having a hard time keeping the so desired customer loyalty.

The prestige leader   The most exclusive. The prestige leader is addressing a small group of customers with expensive products. This is an extreme choice with extreme consequences. Upholding the company image can be rigorous and costly. Rolls Royce is the most obvious example, but also Bang & Olufsen in audio and video equipment. Not many companies claim the prestige leadership, though many companies do have a single product or a product line that aims to be the most exclusive. Examples are the Apple Titanium Powerbook G4 and a company creating 'the most exclusive mobile phones' is Vertu, available in 18 carat gold or platinum. The Vertu mobile phone is not just giving the owner an instrument to call with, it is giving them exclusivity, a way to stand out and above all a confirmation of their status.

The quality leader   The best. This type of company may seem in many ways identical to the prestige leader, but it is not. The best does not necessarily mean the most exclusive. The best means no compromises on quality. In the yearly published list of most reliable cars, Toyota is already for years now the number 1; but it is certainly not an exclusive car. The developers in technology companies tend to opt for being the quality leader. It is against their nature to compromise. But the market for the quality leader is limited and few companies can afford not to compromise. In the IT industry, the quality leader finds its customers in niche markets. Examples are the Canon high-quality digital cameras for professional photography, the Barco Reference Calibrator professional color displays for desktop publishing ('The Reference Calibrator V offers the highest levels of accuracy for colour-critical applications' – according to Barco) and Silicon Graphics workstations for image rendering.

The global leader   The best positioned to serve world markets. The global leader uses its worldwide presence as one of the key benefits. These companies want to be known for their global coverage, mainly for two reasons: (a) to be attractive to multi-nationals or companies that trade on the world market and (b) to be appealing to investors. Examples are Invensys claims to be the global leader in production and resource management, Syntellect positions itself as the global leader in speech recognition applications, Cable and Wireless ('one of the world's leading global communications companies'), AT&T and AOL to mention a few. Products too can claim global leadership, to convince multi-nationals to standardize on them. Worldwide support and localization of the product into many languages must be established. Most of today's IT products are globally available and many companies claim global leadership.

The bargain leader   Offering the lowest price. This type of company is the exact opposite of the prestige leader. Saving money is the top priority, exclusivity and customer service are not. The bargain leader is not the same as the market share leader. A bargain leader can be a one-man shop. This is very clear positioning that can often be found in a company's name, like PayLess or Budget. Tele2, a Finnish telecom provider, is successfully gaining market share by positioning its services as the cheapest. The positioning of PC manufacturer Emachines is the same.

The innovation leader The most creative. This image is tempting for many technology companies that are proud of their creativity and innovative products. But be aware, this market is often limited to other 'techies' and early adaptors. Being an innovation leader can also mean hefty spending on development and research. The biggest threat to the innovation leader is that as soon as an innovative new product gets some market acceptance and is ready to harvest, a competitor will walk away with their success. Examples of innovation leaders are Natural Micro Systems, Xerox and to some extent Philips. Many of the IT companies have a product or a line of products that are positioned as the most innovative. These products do contribute to the company image, but are not always financially successful.

The technology leader The first. Being the first can bring enormous advantages. Technology leaders face little or no competition and can easily create market share. This also means relatively high margins, due to lack of price-fighting. But education and hefty doses of evangelism are required. Examples: Netscape as the first Internet browser, VisiCalc (the first spreadsheet program), SAP (the first ERP software). From VisiCalc, we can learn that it is hard maintaining the leadership. The success of the first spreadsheet attracted others (like Lotus with its 1-2-3) to create a second generation software.

The value leader The best value for money. The value leader often delivers quality with some compromises but good products are always offered at a reasonable price. The consequence is that a company cannot really stand out. These products are not the cheapest, nor the best, nor the most innovative and exclusivity is simply not a factor. But if a value leader can prove that they offer the most for the customer's money, success can come easily. And not being the cheapest, nor the best, can be used as an advantage. Value for money combined with a no-nonsense approach appeals to a large portion of the market. Examples of products claiming value leadership are Epson printers, Goldmine CRM software.

The flexibility leader The most adaptable. Products are essentially made to order. Instead of telling the customer what product to buy and how to use it, the philosophy is; 'tell us what you need and we will create it for you'. Because the customer often deals directly with the company specifying their wishes, this creates a complex production process, often compensated by an efficient distribution channel. Dell is an example of a computer manufacturer claiming the flexibility leadership, enabled by cutting out the retail channel and an almost build-to-order of commodity products. SAP and Aspect are software companies customizing their software and configurations to match the customer needs, using high-skilled consultants. SAP was one of the first companies with personalized web pages (mySAP) and also their pay-off 'the power to build an adaptive business' clearly aims to position themselves as the flexibility leader.

Some of the above company and product identities are mutually exclusive, others can be combined. But the simpler the approach, the easier it is to create an image around it. If you combine identities, make sure your message does not get lost in the process and try to stick to the choices made. In other words, do not confuse target customers by spending money on a glossy brochure if your goal is to be the bargain leader in the market.

The image you create for your product adds to the perceived value in the market and sets the expectations. For example, if a magazine is printed on cheap paper, readers are automatically biased on its content. And wine served from a carton or bottled with a plastic cork is perceived as not as flavorful. The same is true with the packaging, the manuals, the website and everything else you create around your product.

The brand and the image you are creating around your product have to be in line with the company's ambition. The introduction of a cheap BMW can ruin the company's image. This is not what people expect from BMW – *The Ultimate Driving Machine*.

But within the product line or company product portfolio there is room for individual positioning. Is your new product top-of-the-line or is it simply being developed to gain market share? Analyze your ambitions with the product and create your image and brand accordingly.

Step 2: The ideal client

Take a moment to think about the customer you want to reach. Who is your ideal client? Then answer the following questions:

- What is the profession of your ideal client? Is that profession dominantly male, female or is that of no importance?

- Can you say anything about the industry your client is working in or are you targeting consumers? If so, what are their hobbies? What is their age, education level and what are their interests?

- What other technology-oriented products are your client using and for what purpose?

- How much money does the client have to spend? Is your client sensitive to price?

- If you are in the business-to-business market, what is the client's position in the company where they work? Who are you ideally talking to and who will use your product? Who makes the decision on your type of product?

- How big is the company you want as your customer? Think about it in terms of employees and in terms of revenue. Also think in terms of national or multi-national, local, regional or national presence.

- What is the image of your ideal customer? Is your client known for choosing leading edge technology or are they more conservative? Is your client well known and a leader in its own area?

- What keeps the client awake at night? In other words, what are the main concerns? Think about the type of business your client is in, about their business model, the competition, their clients and the problems they are facing.

- Most importantly, what is your product going to do to improve the client's life? What compelling reason does your client have to buy your product?

The importance of describing your ideal customer is that you can create a profile of the prospect you want to address. Realizing what the profile of your ideal customer is makes it easier to direct your communication and marketing efforts in that direction.

Who is your audience?

Your audience is the group of people in which your ideal customer is. Understand that your audiences will most likely change during the life of the product. The first mobile phones were targeted at mobile professionals who perceived a car-phone as a status symbol. Prices were high and the sales volume low. Today, mobile phones are a part of nearly everyone's lives, from children to senior citizens alike. Mobile phone use is not limited to any one function. Prices are now very low and the volumes are accordingly high. In the first phase of the mobile phones, your audience, the people making decisions to buy mobile phones were high up in the company's hierarchy. Today a mobile phone is a commodity. Although it still has more or less the same functionality, the audience changed dramatically.

The above-mentioned change in target audience is described more in detail in Chapter 6.

Step 3: Take a look at the 'whole product'

Regardless of how firmly you believe your product to be the best on the market, it is very unlikely the product itself will stand on its own. It will probably function in an environment alongside other products and it needs complementary services for your customer. Together with the other products and services the whole solution your customer is looking for is formed (Figure 5.1).

Think about compelling reasons why that target customer should buy your product and what other products and services are needed to create a whole solution. By doing so, you will:

- See opportunities for partnering.

- Be prepared to present your product as part of the whole solution the customer is looking for.

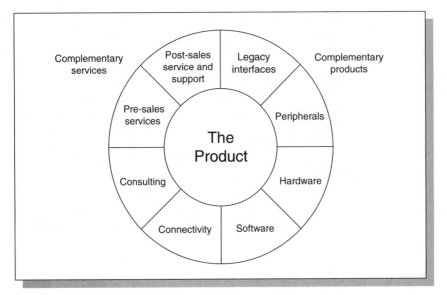

Figure 5.1 The whole product

- Inspire the customer with the possibilities your product offers and explain how you cooperate with partners to create this whole solution.

Computers are obvious examples of products that are just a part of the whole solution. Without the operating system and software, a computer is a useless collection of iron, copper, silicon and other elements. It needs these complementary products. The same is true for software. It is not surprising that most computer vendors team up with software suppliers to ship a system that includes a readily installed operating system as well as numerous applications, games and tools.

In addition to complementary products, the services surrounding the product are often essential for the customer. Software products like SAP and Siebel cannot exist without the consultancy and system integration (SI) offered by others.

When picturing the whole product, try to see things from the customer's perspective. As a customer, what do you want in addition to the product itself? Is a certificate or recommendation from the vendor a crucial part of the solution? What about test results? How important is support? And as a customer, where do I go for support? Where does your customer go for maintenance and repair? How much training is required to use the product and where can I get this training?

If you buy a printer, you want to know what paper it uses, where you can buy ink-cartridges or toner and where to go in case of a problem. A digital photo camera needs memory cards, software for viewing and manipulation, printers, special paper, service and support and even the 'email-and-print' service offered by the drugstore around the corner. These are all part of the whole product.

Make a list of the complementary products and services and look for opportunities to partner with companies delivering the complementary products and services.

Step 4: The unique selling points

The unique selling points of your product are the real differentiators. They are those benefits that cannot be found among the competition. To determine USPs, answer the following questions keeping in mind the whole product:

- What problem does your product solve and for whom?

- How does the product solve the problem? How is this different from the alternatives? Is this a faster solution therefore saving time? Or is it simply more convenient? Does it require less training?

- What 'core competency' does your product have that enables it to be the leading provider of this solution?

- What unique value or sales proposition does your product offer?

- Take a look at the efforts your customer has to take to buy, install and use the product. Do you have a better distribution mechanism than the competition? Will your customer be up-to-speed more easily?

- What unique complementary services and partnerships do you offer to your customer?

- What are the consequences to the customer if they do not buy your product?

Do not answer these questions in terms of features, but in terms of benefits. Does your new digital video camera come with three CCD chips? Why is that a benefit? Can your new accounting software be accessed via the Internet? Why is that an advantage?

Step 5: Leading the analysts

You now know your customer, you have outlined the USPs and have defined your product ambition. Now it is time to get creative and show the world just how different your product is.

Anyone analyzing your product will try to compare it with the products of your competitors. Do not wait for them to come up with criteria for comparison, guide them in the direction you want them to go in. A graphical representation is a powerful way to set your product apart from the competitors. You can plot out the market landscape in such a way that your product is positioned as *best*.

At first glance, you are probably wondering what the coordinate system in Figure 5.2 represent. Well, that is for you to decide! your product has the solution that is best integrated with other software *and* requires the least training? Put it on both axes. Do you offer the best customer service and very high performance? Then that is your coordinate system.

Be creative. You can lead the analysts in the direction that you want.

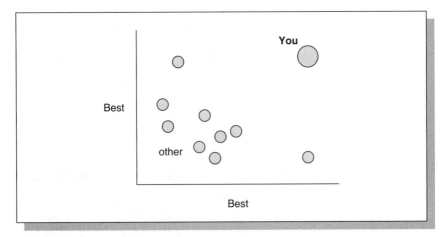

Figure 5.2 Plotting the market landscape

An alternative is to shift the axes, forming four quadrants – especially handy if you want to present your product as a next generation product, a paradigm shift (Figure 5.3).

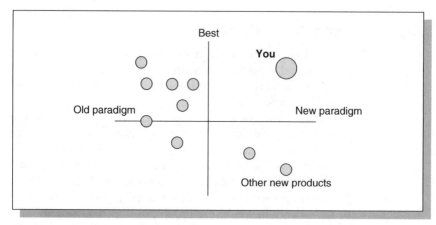

Figure 5.3 Alternative market landscape

Tell the world why your implementation of your second, third or fourth generation of products is better than others.

Example: Say you are introducing a color printer, based on the latest bubblejet technology. The fact that you are using this latest technology, offering a better resolution and thus a sharper image, is the paradigm shift and sets you apart from a big part of the competition. Your printer is not necessarily the fastest, nor is it the cheapest. But the ink-cartridges you use are cheaper and very efficient, resulting in a lower price per page printed. Now you can lead the analysts by creating a market landscape diagram as in Figure 5.3, with the price per page printed on the vertical axis (lowest price at the top, of course). This indicates that all competitors on the left side are using obsolete technology and that your implementation using that new technology is better than the rest.

Step 6: Market segmentation and market attractiveness

It is possible that your product is suitable for many market segments. Do not try to address them all. If you try to reach everybody, fearing that you might miss out on great opportunities, you risk reaching no one. The focus should be on dominating one segment of the market. Once that is accomplished, it is a lot easier to expand to another segment.

When you choose a particular market segment to focus on, it becomes easier to reach your targeted audience. You determine which distribution channels and partners to team up with, and the message is personalized. Choosing a segment of the market helps you create that unique space in the mind of the customer. It also helps the company to define clear goals and creates focus and guidelines to achieve the goals set.

A consumer version of a video camera has many applications. But the prime target still appears to be the typical father or mother with young kids. Almost any parent can recognize that they too would like to be able to make home videos of their children. We have seen this television or print ad before: two parents between the ages of 30 and 40 relishing in their child's first school play or winning goal. For some products, like home video cameras, the target market is clear from the start. But in many cases there are several segments to choose from. This choice is made easier by conducting market segment analysis.

Take another look at your ideal customer and product ambition and then make a list of possible market segments. Here are some examples of how the market can be divided into segments:

- *Company size*: How big is the company of your ideal customer? Some products are specifically useful for the very large enterprises, other products are better suited for Small Office and Home Office (SOHO) or Small and Medium Enterprises (SMEs). Also take into consideration how well your company can deal with either of these segments.

- *Vertical market segment*: Very important when you have a somewhat-specialized product. For example, if you are marketing a professional color printer, possible vertical market segments could be pre-print, design, printing and publishing, and copy shops.

- *Geography*: Sometimes geography is important and can be seen as a segment. Geography can be defined by country or region (like 'France' or 'Los Angeles area'), but it can also be specified as 'rural area' or 'city'.

- *Adoption life cycle stage*: The nature of your product may require a division between 'innovators', 'early adaptors', 'early majority' and 'late majority'. The adoption life cycle and its stages are described in Chapter 6.

- *Business advantage*: The business advantage and the compelling reason to buy your product might differ from customer to customer. The professional color printer in the example above can be purchased to provide a cost-effective color check, but it can also be used for generating revenue with the production of small quantities of posters.

Or it can be any combination of the above.

Now you have listed possible market segments, but the goal is to rank the market segments in terms of attractiveness and make a choice. To assess the attractiveness of the market segments you have listed, you should make a list of criteria that are important to you such as:

- Accessibility of the segment. Some market segments are easier to reach than others because they all read the same magazine. Or perhaps, the number of companies is limited or they have a strong branch organization. 'High schools', as a segment, is rather accessible. 'In-house call centers' as a segment is not because many types of companies can have an in-house call center. Your existing customers, your network and dealer channels are important factors in judging how accessible a segment is.

- The segment has a compelling reason to buy *and* has the available budget. For example, you are releasing a new hand-held computer that is ideal for students. Ask yourself if the price of your product is in line with a limited student budget.

- The segment is not currently well served by competitors. If there are four market segments that you are considering, and one of those is not well served by the competition, this speaks in favor of that segment. Less competition means less price pressure and easier domination.

- The segment will create new opportunities in other segments (a stepping stone). The domination of one sector can be very helpful as a step to an even more attractive market which is harder to reach. Looking again at the professional color printer – if you want to reach the large in-house desktop publishing market, dominance in the pre-press and publishing market is very helpful.

- The segment is small enough to be dominated. Being dominant in at least one segment can be very helpful. Rate your possible market segments on how easy it would be to dominate each one.

The above listed criteria are just some examples.

Enter the market segments and criteria into a matrix and scores in each cell from 1 to 5.

	Segment 1	Segment 2	Segment 3	Segment 4	Segment 5
Criteria 1					
Criteria 2					
Criteria 3					
Criteria 4					
Criteria 5					
Total score					

The total score gives an indication of the most attractive market segment. Feel free to create your own version of the market attractiveness assessment. Perhaps you want to add a weighing factor to the criteria to represent to the importance of that criteria. Use your own judgment, the matrix above is no more than a tool to help you make a choice.

But remember you must make a choice. Do not try to go after all of the market segments at once. Instead create a strategy on how to conquer one market segment at a time.

Step 7: The positioning statement

You now have all of the ingredients necessary to create a powerful positioning statement for your product. This statement clearly explains what it is you are offering and to whom as well as why this product is better than others.

For . . .	[target audience, your ideal customer in your chosen market segment]
Who . . .	[need or opportunity, how will your product improve their lives]
Your product . . .	[product category, based on your whole product analysis]
That provides . . .	[compelling reason for your ideal customer to buy]
Unlike . . .	[competing products]
Our product . . .	[primary differentiation, based on USPs and differentiators and your market landscape analysis]

The above elements are the basis for your positioning statement. A product positioning statement is a powerful way to further define strategy. It is also the basis for product promotion and to create that unique space in the mind of your prospect.

Create your own positioning statement. This should be as short and powerful as possible. You can also team up with marketing communication specialists and, using the above-mentioned elements, work together to create a strong positioning statement.

Television commercials, at least good ones, often are a direct translation of the positioning statement. An advertisement for a new washing powder first shows a man struggling to iron his shirts. A common view in Europe where it is not the habit to bring shirts to the drycleaner for ironing. Then New Dash detergent is introduced to show how the product makes ironing much easier. Once again the man is shown, this time with a big smile on his face, ironing with enthusiasm. Watching this ad, I knew they were talking directly to me. Like many men these days, I always iron my own shirts – mostly done in a rush in the early morning. If this washing powder does indeed make ironing even a little easier, then I am their customer. Everything was addressed in a short commercial: The target audience, the need of the targeted audience and how the product solved this particular need.

By making the choice to specifically address men in a hurry, I clearly recognized myself. They created a unique space in my head. And that is exactly what you need to do with your product positioning.

Conclusions

To win the battle for mind share, you need to carefully position your product, in such a way that you reach the prospects that you want to have as customers, that recognize that you are addressing their needs with your product in a better way than the competition is doing.

Product positioning requires choices and understanding of your target market. By making the choices and methodically creating your product positioning, you will be able to get into a prospect's mind and occupy that space.

Interesting links on the web

About market segmentation

http://cism.bus.utexas.edu/res/articles/segmentation.html

About product positioning

http://www.uiowa.edu/~commstud/adclass/adage-positioning.html
http://en.wikipedia.org/wiki/Positioning_(marketing)

6

The product adoption life cycle

From innovators to laggards

Objectives

This chapter starts again with the product life cycle, but looks at it from a different perspective. It gives you insight about:

1 How the product will appeal to different types of buyers for each phase of the product life cycle? Each group has its own motivation and its own characteristics.

2 How each type of buyer can help you in optimizing your product life cycle?

3 How your knowledge about the product adoption life cycle should be applied to your product marketing strategy and targeted toward the different types of buyers while your product follows the phases of its life cycle.

4 Why 'knowledge-based' companies, such as consultancy firms and system integrators, are an exception to the product adoption life cycle?

During the product life cycle, a product will go from 'new and modern' to 'known and accepted' and finally end up 'outdated and obsolete'. At every stage of the product life cycle, your product appeals to a different group of people. In other words, a different group will adopt your new product. This product adoption life cycle was first described by Thomas Leavitt and again examined in Regis McKenna and Geoffrey A. Moore's *Crossing the Chasm* in which they applied the theory to the ICT industry.

In this chapter we take a look at the technology and product adoption life cycle theory and apply it to the marketing of a product during deployment. Understanding the adoption life cycle allows you to fine-tune your positioning toward the shifting target audience and helps to optimize the business performance of your product (Figure 6.1).

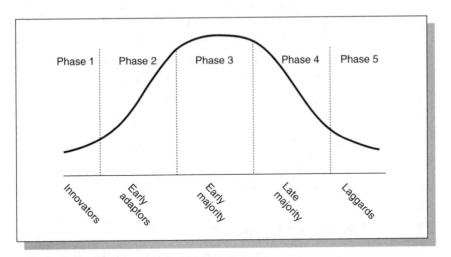

Figure 6.1 Technology and product adoption life cycle

Phase 1: The innovators

In the early stage of a product life cycle, the first group most likely to buy this product is known as the innovators. In the ICT industry this customer can also be characterized as a 'techie'.

The following is a profile of a 'techie':

- A strong aptitude for technical information.

- They enjoy beta testing and are willing to help further develop a product.

- They accept that the product seen as a 'whole product' (see Figure 5.1) is missing elements and not yet in place.

- Driven by an interest in technology and the possibility to learn new things, they are motivated to give important feedback on the product.

'Techies' can be very helpful during the last phase of product development. They can partner with you to perform field tests and can provide essential input from a technical point of view.

The challenges you may face when dealing with this group are:

- 'Techies' are information hungry and will likely demand your full attention. They will probably not want to deal with your sales people, and instead want full access to your engineers.

- Anticipate that at this stage you will make no margin on your product. The 'techies' expect a non-profit deal, or even beta products for free.

The key role of the innovators, or 'techies', is to test-market your product and act as gatekeepers to the early adaptors.

The end of this phase of the product life cycle is often marketed by an official product launch.

Phase 2: The early adaptors

Early adaptors are very important to the success of a product. They are the visionaries – those that recognize the possibilities for a new product or a new technology. Sometimes they can even make or break a new product.

Early adaptors often possess the following characteristics:

- They have a great appreciation and imaginative power for the application of strategic products and developments.

- They are attracted by high risk and potentially high reward propositions.

- They will commit to supplying or helping to fill in missing elements.

- They are motivated by the dramatic competitive advantage they might gain by implementing break-through technologies ahead of their competitors.

- Because their motives are business oriented, they are not very price sensitive.

The early adaptors will likely demand from you:

- Rapid time-to-market. The early adaptor seeks new products that can bring competitive advantages. Being ahead of the competition is a matter of timing.

- A high degree of customization. The early adaptors are visionaries and they have a clear picture of what they want to reach the envisioned competitive advantage.

- Extensive support.

Early adaptors are creative thinkers and can help you put your product on the map! They are often recognized by other companies in your target market and their testimonies provide credibility and enable you to gear up for the next phase. They can help you to fund and develop the market for your product.

Phase 3: The early majority

In the ICT market, the early majority is a pragmatic group that is far less adventurous than the innovators or the early adaptors. But this group is far bigger than both combined.
The early majority has the following characteristics:

- They focus on proven technology and proven applications.

- They carefully watch the early adaptors of their market segment.

- They understand real-world issues and trade-offs.

- They are astute managers and cannot afford to take high risks.

- They like to follow the market leader.
- They can be motivated by sustainable productivity improvements via evolutionary change.

The early majority can also present challenges by:

- Insisting on good references from trusted colleagues.
- Demanding to see the solution in production at a reference site.
- Demanding a finished product with training and customer service already in place.

In the ICT industry, the early majority is truly in the main stream of the market. These are the customers you had in mind when designing the product and this group will determine whether your product will be profitable or not.

Phase 4: The late majority

The late majority in the product adoption cycle is formed by the true conservatives of the market, those slow to accept changes in technology. These 'late bloomers' allow you to extend the life of your product.

Here are some of the characteristics of the late majority:

- They are averse to risk. 'If it still works, don't touch it' is their motto.
- They are better in dealing with people than technology.
- When investing in technology, they rely heavily on a single trusted advisor.
- They are very price sensitive.
- Their prime motivation is just to stay in business.

Your challenge to satisfy this group:

- Deliver completely pre-assembled solutions.
- Provide impeccable help files and flawless functioning of the product.

As a product manager, this group of buyers may not be as interesting or as challenging as the previous groups.

But extending the life cycle of your product can increase the total contribution of that product and create extra revenue through services such as maintenance and training.

Phase 5: The laggards

The laggards in the adoption of ICT products are the skeptics, and can be characterized by the following:

- They are good at debunking marketing hype.

- They do not believe productivity improvement arguments and will try to prove you wrong.

- They like taking a contrary position.

- They seek to block purchases of new technology.

- Their main motivation is to maintain a status quo.

Do the laggards or the skeptics sound like a group of people you want to ignore? From a marketing point of view you should stay clear of this hostile group. They are not your customer base and can actually get in the way of early adoption. Just have your story ready.

The influence on your marketing strategy

Your knowledge of the product and technology adoption cycle should be applied directly to your product marketing strategy. You will see that the positioning statement will differ slightly depending on which phase of the life cycle the product is in and so are the services and the organization around your product.

The change in strategy during the life cycle of your product is indicated in Figure 6.2.

1 Test your product using the critical view of the 'techies'. This allows you to create a beachhead within your target market. But be selective, these first users or testers of your product will be treated more like technology partners than customers.

2 Use your experience with the 'techies' to approach the visionaries of your target market. Try to dominate a niche and create, together with these new partners, the whole product. Ask your visionary customers to act as

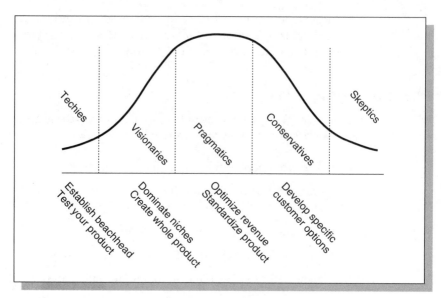

Figure 6.2 Marketing strategy from the adoption life cycle

a reference and give testimonials. At this stage your ideal customer is the influential front-runner. Pamper them – it will pay off during the later phases.

3 The successful implementations with the visionaries are the proof of concept needed to be successful with the large group of pragmatics. You can concentrate on optimizing your revenue and standardize your product offering in terms of configuration, pricing and customer support.

4 If you have succeeded with the pragmatics, you have most likely established a known and proven product-brand in your target market. The product life can be extended to create new configurations or bundles sold at an attractive price.

5 Do not waste any marketing attention at the skeptics.

The exception: Knowledge-based companies

For knowledge-based companies offering services such as SI or consultancy, the marketing strategy based on the product adoption life cycle looks different. This is due to the fact that they are advising other companies on how to implement products for Innovators, Early Adaptors, Early Majority or the Late Majority.

Each of these categories requires a different approach and skills inside the SI or consultancy firm – from the very high skilled and technically educated for the innovators techies to the more straightforward helping hand for the conservatives. The strategy for the knowledge-based companies is to 'swim upstream' (Figure 6.3): Keep the knowledge level adequate for the chosen customer type, which is the target market for the SI, but stay at that target market at that stage in the product adoption life cycle.

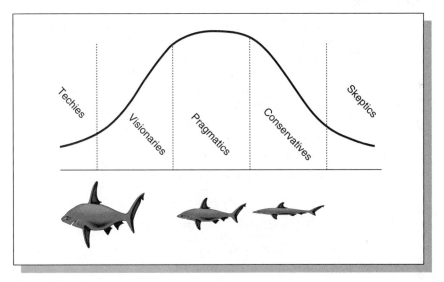

Figure 6.3 Swim upstream

Just like a fish that has to swim against the current to stay at the same place, the system integrators and consultants have to constantly learn and put energy in staying at the same place, serving their chosen category of customers. Take for instance a system integrator focusing on the visionaries of the industry. They have to be as knowledgeable as the visionaries themselves and they have to be able helping the visionaries implement a rather newly introduced product. A product that, as we have learned, often is not fully documented yet and for which training and knowledge in the market is scarce. The relationship they build with their customers is based on their special skills and their being ahead of the rest of the market. Their target market is rather limited, but their knowledge justifies high hourly rates. To keep up these rates and to keep their customers satisfied, they constantly have to learn about the new products and technologies coming out. Products that move to the next phase of the product life cycle are no longer of their interest. So knowledge-based services always focus on the same type of customers, staying at the same place of the product life cycle. As if they are swimming upstream.

Conclusions

The profile of the customers buying your product will vary during the life cycle of the product. When the product changes from new and innovative to accepted and mature to finally outdated, the audience that is attracted to your product will change accordingly.

You as the product manager need to understand these different types of customers:

1 The innovators (the 'techies').

2 The early adaptors (the visionaries).

3 The early majority (the pragmatics).

4 The late majority (the conservatives).

5 The laggards (the skeptics).

Understanding these different types of buyers and their motivation allows you to better manage and optimize the product life cycle of your product.

Interesting links on the web

http://www.valuebasedmanagement.net/methods_rogers_innovation_
adoption_curve.html
http://www.zonalatina.com/Zldata99.htm

CHAPTER 7

The product launch

Prepare, plan and execute

Objectives

The objective of this chapter is to give you the tools to prepare for the launch of your product. You will learn how to:

1 Set your objectives for the launch.

2 Plan the product launch, including a checklist for all materials needed.

3 Decide whether you need different events for different target groups such as press, dealers, customers and the internal organization, with considerations on how to approach these different groups.

The chapter ends with some words on the promotion of your product.

You never have a second chance to make a first impression. The big kick-off of your product had better be good. No matter what type of product you are bringing to market, the launch is an important milestone and needs a lot more attention than just giving the sales department the green light to go out and begin hunting for customers.

The product launch needs thorough planning, excellent preparation and a first-rate execution. The best way to begin is by setting your goals.

Setting the objectives

The goal seems fairly obvious: To successfully launch your product and reach your target market through sales channels and the press. But when is a launch considered to be successful? How do you measure success? It is important to be specific when setting your goals. This straightforward approach, referred to as SMART objectives, helps to clearly define the goals of your product launch:

S = Specific
M = Measurable
A = Achievable
R = Relevant
T = Time framed

For example, terms like 'good' and 'successful' need to be specified in a way that can be measured. If they are measurable, they can be evaluated afterward. And be sure not to make the frequent mistake of setting your objectives too high. Ask yourself with each objective whether it is relevant or not. For example an objective such as 'Have 15 press representatives visiting the press conference' is not relevant. What is important is what the press does with that information.

The objective should also be time framed, indicating when the desired result should be reached. So, let us say you are introducing a new type of flat screen that interacts with a stylus as pointing device. The device can lay flat on a desk and is designed for creating artwork within desktop publishing applications.

Here are some SMART objectives to set for the product launch:

- Press articles appear in at least 4 out of 8 computer and desktop publishing magazines within the first four weeks after launch.

- At least 90 percent of all dealers in the retail channel will order your product for their stock within the first week after launch.

- Finally 100 percent of your own sales representatives and 75 percent of the sales representatives from your indirect sales channel are able to name at least three USPs of the new screen and stylus.

In the example above, you could argue that the appearance of press articles should be better specified as 'positive articles'. But 'positive press articles' is no longer specific, for who decides when a press article is positive or not? If it is unclear how to interpret the word 'positive', then you can better leave it out.

Planning for the product launch

You have set your SMART objectives, and know precisely what you want to achieve. Now you must develop a plan to help achieve those goals. Treat your product launch as a project and set up a project plan with actions, a timeline and a budget.

There are three basic categories of things to plan in your product launch project plan:

1 The creation of materials needed.

2 The planning and organization of launch events.

3 The promotion around the product launch.

Materials needed

Since every product is different, it is of course up to the product manager to decide exactly what is needed for the introduction. The following is a suggested list of materials needed:

- *Price lists* with suggested retail prices, dealer discounts, volume discounts or other price-related conditions.

- *Pricing tool*: When you have a complex product, with many options and/or possible configurations, a pricing tool is an extremely helpful instrument and can be easily created in Excel.

- *Requirements*: What are the minimum technical requirements your product needs to function?

- *List of USPs and main differentiators*: You have created this list already in your product positioning.

- *Product description*: A description of your product in 600, 300 and 100 words, and a one-liner. These text blocks can be used for articles, press releases, proposals and other written items.

- *Press release(s)*: Your PR agency or in-house PR people need to be briefed on what you want as the main message to come across. Think about the type of press people you want to reach. You might have to create different press releases. A journalist of a specialized IT magazine will be triggered by other USPs than a journalist of a daily newspaper. The first one is likely to be more interested in the new possibilities your product offers and the technology used, while the latter one most likely wants to know more about your forecast and what your product does for the company.

- *White paper*: This document will act as a brochure for the visionaries. A white paper should describe the vision and technology behind a product from the conceptual point of view.

- *Product brochure*: If you decide that a product brochure would be beneficial, brief the marketing communication department or those in charge of creating these materials. Start with the product positioning statement and make sure to include all of the work you have done on targeting and positioning.

- *Product datasheet*: This should include features and benefits, technical details and requirements.

- *Sales pitch presentation and, if needed, a presentation for dealers*: These two are not the same. The presentation for sales is strictly to help sales representatives present the product to prospects. The dealer presentation is designed to motivate the dealer to take on your product and sell it for you. The dealer presentation should especially focus on benefits for the dealer.

- *Frequently Asked Questions (FAQs) and answers*: The FAQ document is important for customer service people and can be used as background information for sales and press. It may be wise to create several FAQs for different target groups.

- *Information on the competition*: How do they position themselves? What are their strengths and weaknesses? And what do you know about their marketing and pricing strategies in order to better sell against them? This information is, of course, confidential and for internal use only.

- *Market background information*: What is the target market and what are their day-to-day issues and needs? Who are the big or influential players in the market?

- Sales remuneration plan (if applicable).

- *Sales training and sales support training*: If possible, involve yourself in sales training.

- *Training* for customer service, installation, operations or any other involved departments.

- *Product demonstration kit or instructions for product demonstrations*: Line out a script and make sure that the person giving demonstrations knows how to trigger and keep the attention of the prospect. Make sure the focus is on compelling reasons to buy the product.

- *Any promotional material* that supports the brand and sales of your product. Posters, danglers, wobblers, screensavers and other give-aways and tools to attract attention for your product.

Think about the materials needed and make your list. Assign responsibilities and budgets, add a timeline and enter this into your project launch plan.

Launch events: Some important considerations

Are you creating events around the launch of your product, and if so, what type, how big should it be and who do you want to reach? All of this should be decided based on the SMART objectives you have defined.

Here are some considerations.

Sneak preview for press

Before the official launch, arrange to preview your product for a select group of journalists. Invite between two and a maximum of five journalists, preferably one at a time. This should be organized one to two weeks before the official press conference and those invited should be from non-competing outlets. Invite, for instance, someone from a magazine specialized in your market segment, another from a more general ICT magazine and maybe a journalist from a daily newspaper or lifestyle magazine. It is preferable to invite journalists with whom you have a personal and trusted relationship.

The advantages of giving sneak previews are:

- You can test the message you want to convey with a small audience. This is an excellent way to prepare for the official introduction. Take notice of how they react to your story and your product demonstration. This will give you a clear indication of which features and benefits excite them and which part of your story is not clear enough. This also lets you know which questions to expect during the press conference.

- This is perhaps the best chance you have to get press coverage. The fact that you have selected these journalists for a special session motivates them to publish a story their competitors do not yet have.

- By giving these selected journalists a sneak preview, it is likely the article will be published at the time of introduction.

If possible, prepare an agreement for each journalist, which includes a non-disclosure form and an embargo on publishing until the official launch date. You might also consider leaving some information, such as pricing, out.

Sneak preview for selected visionary companies

Remember that the visionary companies are your early adaptors and act as a gatekeeper to the early majority, or the pragmatists in your market segment. Their opinion on your new product is vital. They are special to you and you can let them know by allowing them to 'test-drive' a production version of your product. This should only be done under the condition that they provide constructive feedback on the product and that you will be allowed to quote them at product launch. A good quote from a visionary company is powerful testimony.

Press conference

The press conference should be organized by your PR and marketing communication people. A product presentation for members of the press is not the same as a sales pitch presentation. Most press people consider sales-oriented arguments as 'rubbish'. They might also be given the feeling they are not being taken seriously. Think about who will be attending the press conference and make sure you address all of their interests. So the specialist magazine not only wants to know about the benefits, but also the applied technology. If someone from the lifestyle press is attending, then you must also pay attention to the more human aspects of your product, such as design and trends in the market. All members of the press want to know about performance of the company and expectations for the product.

Always take the press seriously and let them know that you take them seriously. Work together with PR to create a well-prepared presentation. The press conference should be attended by you as well as senior management, such as Director of Marketing, the CEO or General Manager and the CFO or Financial Director.

When creating press materials make it as easy as possible for a journalist to publish an article about your product. Provide a full package containing a press release, product documentation, white paper, product positioning statement and any other valuable documentation in both hard copy and soft copy. Include any relevant company information and do not forget the full-color photo!

If possible, have some evaluation units ready. And practice! Practice your presentation and practice your demonstration. No matter how experienced you are at giving presentations, never step in front of the press without having your presentation practiced with some audience. It will increase your confidence, your timing and your whole performance.

Sales introduction

With the sales team you must do whatever it takes to get the sales people excited. Create enthusiasm and motivate them to go out there and sell your product. Whether you use music, sound effects or humor, make sure your introduction is a real show with a lot of fun and fuss.

Unique selling points and background information on the target customer are also important, but do not forget to explain to sales people exactly what is in it for them, especially how much easier you have made life for them. Present the promotional campaign, price lists and pricing tools and give them easy access to any relevant marketing materials.

The introduction of a new product to the sales force is always a great moment to honor the entire team that helped realize the product. If possible, this event should be a company-wide happening. A good excuse for a party.

Dealer event

If you already have an established dealer channel, the introduction of your new product can be combined with the sales team event. But there are some advantages to hosting a separate event for dealers:

- You can concentrate your message around their needs. The 'what is in it for them' is different for a dealer than for your own sales force.

- It is important to inform your own sales force before the dealers themselves are introduced to your product. This allows your sales force to answer any questions the dealers might have. Plus, you already have the sales team on your side, adding to the enthusiasm.

- Information provided to the sales force about the competition is probably not the same information you want to give to dealers.

- Last but not least, the dealer event should be more than 'just' a product introduction. It is an excellent opportunity to get them more committed to your company and give them the confidence that they are real partners and not just a sales outlet.

Customer event

Never ignore the customer base you already have. If you think your new product is suitable for existing customers, inviting them to special events can be a very effective sales method.

Here are some tips:

- If possible, use an external, well-respected party or person to testify how well your product addresses the needs of the market.

- Always include your sales people in a customer-oriented event. When going through a dealer channel, set up a roadshow and enlist the help of dealers.

- Create extra time for networking. Sales representatives need time to get to know their customers and spend valuable time with them. A customer event is also an excellent opportunity to meet the users of your products.

The promotion

I am not going to spend too much time on the promotion of your product – enough books have already been written on this subject. Here are just a few key points on promoting your product.

Feed the company website and make sure people can find your information on the Internet.

Spend your money wisely. Test your campaign. Do not rent an expensive booth at an exhibition, just because your competitors will be there. Only do this if it looks like the company will profit in some way. Treat a promotional campaign like a business plan: Compare the investment needed with the expected profit.

Carefully choose the promotional medium that best addresses your ideal customer in your target market. Mistakes made can sometimes prove to be very expensive.

For example, when the energy market was first privatized in the Netherlands in 1999, a start-up company called energiebedrijf.com took the opportunity to start selling electricity to the top 500 energy-consuming companies in the Dutch market. They created a beautiful website and promoted their newborn company through radio advertisements. Sure enough, they received hundreds of phone calls and requests for information from all over the country. The problem was that only four of these requests came from prospects in their target market. The majority of calls came from residential users and small companies. Energiebedrijf.com eventually changed its promotion strategy and hired a direct marketing company to approach their 500 target customers. After this change in direction, the company was able to sign up 60 companies in less than two months.

Conclusions

The launch of your product is an important milestone that needs meticulous preparation that starts with setting the goals for the launch.

There are always three groups you want to convince; your product deserves their attention:

1 Those who will sell the product: sales, dealers, distributors, Value Added Reseller (VARS) and others.

2 Those who you want to buy your product: the customers and members of your target market.

3 Those who have an influence on your target market: the press, analysts and consultants.

It is the kick-off for the sales people to start selling. They need to be well equipped, well informed and above all well motivated. The launch of your product is also an excellent opportunity to create free publicity.

Interesting links on the web

http://www.npd-solutions.com/launchcons.html
http://www.nickwebb.com/Keys6.html
http://www.marketingtactics.com/English/Clients/Philips_LMS/
NCTP_Launch_Plan_OCT1997.pdf
http://www.eclicktick.com/launchchecklist.htm

CHAPTER 8

Cost price calculations

When is a product profitable?

Objectives

The main objective of this chapter about cost price calculations is to show you that calculating the cost of a product is not as straightforward as it seems. In this chapter you will learn:

1 Elements that go into a cost price calculation can be interpreted in many ways.

2 Different methods of calculation will give you very different results and can lead to opposite conclusions about the profitability of your product.

3 Guidelines for a fair calculation of your cost price.

Calculation examples using the same parameters but different methods will clearly show you the remarkable differences in the outcome.

In order to determine how profitable your product is or will be, a firm cost price calculation is crucial. But calculating the cost price of a product takes more than a spreadsheet with product components entered into it.

This chapter will help you with some of the difficulties you are likely to encounter when doing a cost price calculation. Included are different methods, their pros and cons along with practical examples.

Here are some key questions to ask yourself when creating cost price calculations.

- What are the elements that go into a cost price calculation?

- Should product development be entered as assets? Or only partially?

- What should I do with overhead costs?

- How and when do I re-value stock?

The elements in a cost price calculation

There are two basic cost categories:

1 Variable costs

2 Fixed costs.

Variable costs are pretty straightforward. They represent all of the elements included in the product that have a cost attached to them.

- Components (materials), including a percentage for waste.

- Assembly, only if directly related to the individual products.

- Packaging materials, including a percentage for waste.

- Storage costs, only those directly related to the individual products.

Some people might argue that sales commissions and the cost of distribution and shipping should also be included in the variable cost of a product. In my view, these elements are tied to cost of sales and should not contaminate the cost price. These types of costs are related to the creation of revenue and not the production of the product.

Variable costs normally do not cause problems. It is the fixed costs that often ignite all kinds of discussions.

Here are some examples of elements that should be listed under fixed costs:

- Investments made to develop the product

- Investments made in order to produce the product

- Investments made in order to distribute the product

- Marketing materials and cost of the product launch

- Costs for employees directly related to the product

- Interest on loans related to the product

- Overhead.

This all is not as easy and straightforward as it might appear. While it might be simple to determine what all of these costs are, it is not yet clear what portion of these costs should be assigned to your product and over what period those costs should be spread out (depreciation).

Let us take a look at some hypothetical situations:

Example 1   You work for a small software company that creates garden design solutions, targeted at horticulturists. The program can plot the designed garden in 2D, transform it into a 3D impression and has access to a database of plants and possible pavements connected to it. Everything is designed and developed in-house except the database for which you have a license agreement with a third party.

Parameters   Development time: Six months for two FTEs (Full Time Equivalents = the equivalent of two employees working full time). Cost per FTE, including everything required to do their job: €100K per year. After the product is finished, the company expects a need of 0.2 development FTE for maintenance and updates.

Database   €30K for the first year; €3K per year for the following years.

The production (on CD-ROM, in a full-color box with hard-copy manual) is fully outsourced. Hundred copies for €8.5 per product.

Cost for launch activities and marketing materials: €25K.

The company expects to sell 400 copies within the first year of introduction and another 500 copies in the second year at a retail price of €450.

The company markets two other products with a stable total revenue of €1200K per year. You are the only product manager, and your total cost per year is €150K. The total overhead cost of the company per year (housing, directors, finance) equals €600K.

How do you calculate the cost price of your product? If you try to enter everything into a spreadsheet, you will immediately face some problems:

- Do you assume all development costs in the first year or do you enter it as an asset and depreciate the cost over the economic lifetime of the product?

- The same problem applies to the purchase of the database and the product launch and development costs.

- How much of the overhead cost should be assigned to your new product and what portion of your own costs?

The traditional method for cost calculation, and the method most likely favored by your financial director, is to spread out all investments over the expected economic lifetime of the product and assign x percent overhead cost to the product, where x = product revenue/total revenue. Your cost calculation would work out as shown in Figure 8.1.

From Figure 8.1 we conclude: The product is not profitable, generating a total loss of €74K, so this product should not go into production. And although this conclusion seems very clear, it can be viewed in a different way.

In the calculation of the cost price of the new product, 13 percent of the overhead of the company has been assigned to it. But is that really fair? 'Yes', the finance people will most likely say because the products of the company must also pay for overhead costs.

This is absolutely true. But what if the introduction of the new product does not affect the overhead costs? The calculation in Figure 8.1 looks very different if we take the overhead cost out as shown in Figure 8.2.

Software company Garden-Help

Economic lifetime	2 years
Retail price	450 Euro
Forecast year 1	400 pieces
Forecast year 2	500 pieces

Investments	In (unit)	Cost per unit	No. of units	Total
Development	Year	100 000	1	100 000
Database	licence	30 000	1	30 000
Product launch		25 000	1	25 000
			Sum of investments:	155 000

Fixed costs per year				
Maintenance	Year	100 000	0.2	20 000
Product management	Year	150 000	0.33	49 500
Overhead	Year	600 000	13%	75 701
Database licence	Year	3 000	1	3 000
			Sum of fixed costs:	148 201

Variable cost			
Manufacturing	unit		20.0
Shipping	unit		10.0
Billing & collecting	unit		1.2
	Total variable cost:		31.2

Profit calculation	Year 1	Year 2	Total
Number of products sold	400	500	900
Revenue	180 000	225 000	405 000
Depreciated investment	77 500	77 500	155 000
Variable cost	12 480	15 600	28 080
Fixed cost	148 201	148 201	296 402
Profit (loss)	(58 181)	(16 301)	(74 482)

Figure 8.1 Cost price calculation example 1

Instead of trying to calculate the entire profit/loss of the product, as if it were an independent business unit, the calculation in Figure 8.2 shows the contribution of the product to the Profit and Loss (P&L) statement for the whole company. And guess what? The product does make a positive contribution. When this product is introduced, and if the forecast is met, it affects the P&L of the company positively by €77K over a two-year period.

And what about your cost as the product manager? In both examples, one-third of your cost has been assigned to this product, given the fact that the new garden design product is one of the three products you

Alternative

Fixed costs per year	In (unit)	Cost per units	No. of units	Total
Maintenance	Year	100 000	0.2	20 000
Product management	Year	150 000	0.33	49 500
Database licence	Year	3 000	1	3 000
			Sum of fixed costs:	72 500

Variable cost		
Manufacturing	unit	20.0
Shipping	unit	10.0
Billing & collecting	unit	1.2
	Total variable cost:	31.2

Contribution	Year 1	Year 2	Total
Number of products sold	400	500	900
Revenue	180 000	225 000	405 000
Variable cost	12 480	15 600	28 080
Depreciated investment	77 500	77 500	155 000
Fixed cost	72 500	72 500	145 000
Profit (loss)	17 520	59 400	76 920

Figure 8.2 Cost price calculation example 2

handle. But does the introduction of this new product increase the cost related to you and your job? If not, then the cost related to you should also be taken out of the equation.

Development of software is a whole different discussion. If the developers were hired specifically to develop this piece of software, then you have no other option than to add the €100K involved in the development of investments needed. But what if you only had to hire one extra developer, for the company and you had the other developer already on the payroll for maintaining and supporting your other products? In that case, the one developer can be seen as part of the overhead cost (this person is required anyway to keep the company going, you just make better use of his presence) and the cost for the newly hired developer goes into your cost price calculation, as it is a clear additional cost spent to realize the new product.

To make this even more complex, you have to ask yourself the question: To what extent can development for the new software be used in other products? To give one example, this new Garden Design software package is targeted at horticulturists. A next product, very similar to this 'professional' software, can be targeted at the consumer/hobby market. This perhaps requires additional help files, templates and examples, but a substantial part of the software can be re-used. In that case, you have good arguments to only assign, let us say 70 percent of the development costs to the professional version and 30 percent to the consumer version.

Your cost calculation looks better and better and you have solid reasons to take out many of the 'sunken' costs, in favor of your product. But how about the risks? The investments needed for the creation of the software is depreciated over a period of two years. This seems to be a relatively short period, but the ICT market is a risky one. If you are able to create your fantastic software in only six months, then the competition can do the same. Therefore, it is wiser to take all investments needed immediately in the first year. No depreciation.

To make the cost discussion as clear as possible, I suggest:

- Do not assign overhead costs to individual products. This often leads to wrong conclusions. Instead, calculate the contribution the product makes to the company or to the business unit of the company.

- Only involve those costs in your cost price calculation that are caused by adding the product to your portfolio. All other costs are 'sunken' and belong to overhead costs or to the costs of a product family, but not to individual product.

- Take all investment costs in the first year after introduction. It prevents building up a legacy and makes risk control easier.

If we apply the above rules to our example, the cost and contribution calculation is as shown in Figure 8.3.

So, after rethinking the initial cost price and profit analysis of Example 1, which resulted in a total loss of €58K in the first year and €74.5K cumulative in two

Software company Garden-Help

Economic lifetime	2 years
Retail price	450 Euro
Forecast year 1	400 pieces
Forecast year 2	500 pieces

Investments	In (unit)	Cost per units	No. of units	Total
Development	Year	100 000	0.35	35 000
Database	licence	30 000	1	30 000
Product launch		25 000	1	25 000
			Sum of investments:	90 000

Fixed costs per year				
Maintenance	Year	100 000	0.2	20 000
Product management	Year	150 000	0	–
Database licence	Year	3 000	1	3 000
			Sum of fixed costs:	23 000

Variable cost		
Manufacturing	unit	20.0
Shipping	unit	10.0
Billing & collecting	unit	1.2
	Total variable cost:	31.2

Contribution calculation	Year 1	Year 2	Total
Number of products sold	400	500	900
Revenue	180 000	225 000	405 000
Investment	90 000	–	90 000
Variable cost	12 480	15 600	28 080
Fixed cost	23 000	23 000	46 000
Contribution	54 520	186 400	240 920

Figure 8.3 Cost price calculation example 3

years, we now have a calculation showing a positive and promising contribution of €54.5K in the first year and cumulative contribution €241K after two years.

Conclusions

When you do your cost price calculations, you have to think very carefully about what you will, and will not, add into the equation. As shown in this chapter, this is not an exact science. Keep it as clean as possible and create for yourself a best and worst case scenario, in order to analyze the risks you and the company are taking. Be prepared to defend the choices you made to the finance people.

Will the cost price and contribution analysis of example 3 be enough for you to convince the rest of the company? The answer is most likely not. The BEP and ROI calculations should not be lacking.

Interesting links on the web

http://www.infomipyme.com/Docs/GT/empresarios/exportar/costoprecio.htm

CHAPTER 9

Finance for non-financials

Introducing BEP and ROI

Objectives

Some understanding of financial calculations is essential to the product manager. The objective of this chapter is to provide you some basic but very valuable background and examples in Excel spreadsheets. The subjects are:

1 What is BEP and how to calculate it?

2 A definition for the Cash Flow.

3 How to conduct an ROI analysis?

4 What is the Net Present Value?

5 Ideas and examples for setting up your forecast.

The Break Even Point

No, I am not trying to insult you by explaining what BEP is. I know you know what that means, or at least I hope you do! The fact is, I wanted this book to be a complete guide to product marketing. So at the risk of turning off readers like you, I decided to include the BEP formula anyway.

Break Even Point is the number of products you have to sell, as the phrase says, to break even. Anything below that means a loss, anything above that number is profit.

Here is the formula:

$$BEP = \frac{\text{Sum of fixed costs}}{(\text{Price per product} - \text{variable cost})}$$

Using the parameters of Figure 8.3, the BEP for the Garden Design software is given below.

$$BEP = 113\,000/(450 - 31.2) = 269.8$$

So at least 270 products need to be sold in order to break even within the first year. The expected sales volume for the first year is set at 400, so even if you miss the forecast by 30 percent, except perhaps for your ego and motivation, the company does not get hurt.

The BEP analysis is an easy way to calculate what is needed to earn back the money you invested. It should not only be applied to the product itself, but also when you consider a marketing campaign, launching an event, hiring new staff or other significant investments.

The Return on Investment

In terms of finance, this is one of the most important indicators. And probably the one thing that your finance manager loses sleep over! It clearly explains what you have done, or will do, with the money. The ROI also helps determine whether it is wise to invest in your project or in something else.

For a short period, it seemed that nearly every company that went public was only interested in 'shareholder value' in an effort to drive up the value of the stock, and of course, employee held stock options. Happily that period is over, and now the 'old-fashioned' steering mechanism of ROI is back in favor.

In deciding where to invest a company's money, or for what project he will agree to commit a loan, the finance manager has a range of options. There may be several ideas for new products, plans for marketing campaigns or potential investments in equipment, housing, manufacturing and so on. The finance manager also has the option of investing in other companies, buying shares or simply putting the money in the bank to accumulate interest. The last option is certainly the safest, but this is not why we are in business. The best way to compare these options is to look carefully at the ROI calculation.

The ROI calculation for a one-year project is quite simple. Compare the cash flow generated by the investment with the investment itself.

Cash flow: the actual movement of money within a company

Using the example of the Garden Design software from Figure 8.3, the ROI for the first year can be calculated as shown in Figure 9.1. A very healthy ROI indeed!

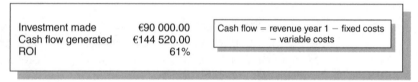

Investment made	€90 000.00	Cash flow = revenue year 1 − fixed costs
Cash flow generated	€144 520.00	− variable costs
ROI	61%	

Figure 9.1 Simple ROI example

But things get a lot more complicated when you have to do an ROI calculation where the pay back of the investment is spread over multiple years. Despite disastrous losses, telecom companies continue to make huge investments in infrastructure, licenses and equipment, on which they base their services. These services will have to generate revenue for multiple years in order to justify the initial investment made. Not that long ago, telecom companies used to depreciate investments made in infrastructure over a period of 25 years. Imagine spreading out an investment over that timeframe! The calculation for that type of ROI is not nearly as straightforward as what is described in Figure 9.1.

Keep in mind, you cannot compare €1 that you spend this year with €1 that you will receive two years from now. You have to work with the Net Present Value (NPV) of that €1 you expect to receive in the future. In order to calculate the NPV of the current and future cash flow, you need to know what the discount rate is. You can use the official discount rate used by banks, but it is best to ask your finance department for the discount rate they use.

The ROI is the discount rate for which the NPV of the investment and the following cash flow equals zero

The ROI is the discount rate for which the NPV of the investment and the following cash flow equals zero. In other words, the rate where the NPV of all future incoming cash flow equals the investment.

Let us build a small example (Figure 9.2). You want to introduce two new services, and in this example they are simply called Service 1 and Service 2. First, you must invest in some machinery or infrastructure; a total investment of €3 million. Because none of the services are introduced at the same time, so you will have to make a forecast for five years.

Investment	€3 000.00						
Year	**1**	**2**	**3**	**4**	**5**	**Total**
Cost service 1	200	210	250	150	70	880
Cost service 2	–	500	400	450	300	1 650
Revenue service 1	800	850	1 050	600	–	3 300
Revenue service 2	–	–	700	1 000	1 200	2 900
Result	600	140	1 100	1 000	830	3 670

Figure 9.2 ROI example 2a

At first sight, the total result does not look too bad: $3670 - 3000 = 670 = 22$ percent of the initial investment.

But this is without taking into account that, the future results cannot be compared one-to-one with the investment you are making today. We should have instead calculated the NPV.

The formula for the NPV is:

$$\text{NPV} = \sum_{i=1}^{n} \frac{\text{values}_i}{(1 + \text{rate})^i}$$

in which:

values = the cash flows in each period

i = the period (in our example, the years)

n = the number of periods

rate = the discount rate

It is good to understand this formula and realize what it does, but this can also be easily done using a spreadsheet program, such as MS Excel. From Figure 9.2 the NPV calculation is shown in Figure 9.3.

Investment	€3 000.00					
Discount	8.00%					
Year	1	2	3	4	5	Total
Cost service 1	200	210	250	150	70	880
Cost service 2	–	500	400	450	300	1 650
Revenue service 1	800	850	1 050	600	–	3 300
Revenue service 2	–	–	700	1 000	1 200	2 900
Result	600	140	1 100	1 000	830	3 670
NPV	€2 848.71		Formula used: = NPV (discount, result1:result5)			

Figure 9.3 ROI example 2b

The conclusion is that with a discount rate of 8 percent, the NPV of the generated cash flow is less than the initial investment. Your financial manager will not be content with this result!

But it still does not explain what the ROI is. You only know that it is less than 8 percent, like the definition said, it is the discount rate giving an NPV of the results that is equal to the initial investment. When you put Figure 9.3 in a spreadsheet, you can play with the discount rate until the number representing the NPV equals €3 000. If you do so, you will find out that the discount rate, in other words the ROI, in the above example is 6.287 percent. This is called an iterative process.

Again, an easy formula in MS Excel helps us here. Although it is not hard to find the ROI by changing the discount rate until you have the desired result, the internal rate of return formula (IRR) does this iterative process for you. In order to use the formula, you have to put the investment as the first of a series of values, the rest of the series being the cash flow results in the years to come (Figure 9.4).

The financial manager of your company will likely demand an ROI of at least 14 percent.

The example given in Figure 9.4 is not very complex, but the method for the ROI calculation is the same – no

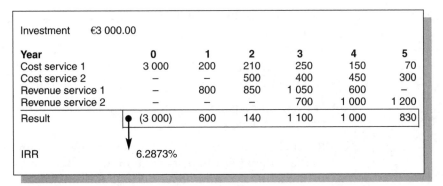

Figure 9.4 ROI example 2c

matter how much more cost and revenue lines you add to the equation. When preparing your financial paragraph of your product plan, an ROI calculation as shown in Figure 9.4 will convince the financial director (with a better rate of course!) that you have done your home work. One additional element is that you need to work out in detail, is your forecast.

The forecast

No one can teach you how to predict the volume of products you are going to sell in the years or even months to come. This is entirely dependent on your ability to judge the potential of your product, the market potential, the capability and expertise of your sales force and the capacity of manufacturing, distribution and/or installation.

The creation of a forecast needs a lot of attention because the initial forecast is the vital input for the ROI calculation and it represents the expectation. After the launch of the product, the forecast becomes a tool for tracking and evaluating results.

It is up to you to create a forecast that is:

- Ambitious, yet realistic. A forecast that is too easy to match will create laziness, but if you set your goals too high, it can be de-motivating.

- An instrument for you and sales, to be used as a tracking tool for manufacturing, distribution and installation and for planning.

- A basis for finance to create cash flow analysis.

Therefore, the main elements of your forecast should contain:

- Forecast in numbers (the volume) of both the product and services related to the product sold.

- Forecast in revenue, of both the product and services related to the product.

- Product shipments. This is not necessarily the same as the number of products sold. Products need to be manufactured and at some periods of the year, the plant or engineers creating the products are at peak performance and delivery times are affected. In most situations, this also implies that the moment you can send out the invoice is affected and so is the cash flow.

- Product invoicing (the finance people will love you for this!). As mentioned above, the moment of invoicing often depends on the moment of shipment. In many occasions, the invoicing is split into several parts, for instance, in case of a custom-build solution or SI project. It is not uncommon to send an invoice at order-acceptance, a second one at installation and a final invoice after testing and customer acceptance. Putting this into the forecast will help the finance people in their cash flow analysis.

- Accumulated figures of the elements above, often called the 'year-to-date' figure. Thus you have your numbers not only per period, but also total up to that period.

It is not that difficult to create a forecast as specified above, it simply requires some fumbling around with a spreadsheet. Make sure (as you, no doubt, always do with every spreadsheet you create) that all the parameters you use are not directly typed into the formulas, but specified in cells that you can refer to at any time.

There are many ways of putting a spreadsheet like that together. But let me give you an example that you may find useful: Let us say your company developed a highly advanced and specialized piece of software for email marketing. It requires industrial PCs equipped with fancy compact PCI cards and you are bringing the total solution to market.

Here are the parameters:

Average system price (×1000)	270
Average revenue for services sold with the system (×1000)	30
Maintenance fee (per year)	15%
Average delivery time	3 months
Gross margin (retail price – variable cost)	71%
Invoicing details:	
At order	40%
At installation	40%
At acceptance	20%

Enter all of the parameters into a spreadsheet, preferably on a special tab called 'parameters', and you can build your forecast (for readability purposes only six months are shown) as shown in Figure 9.5.

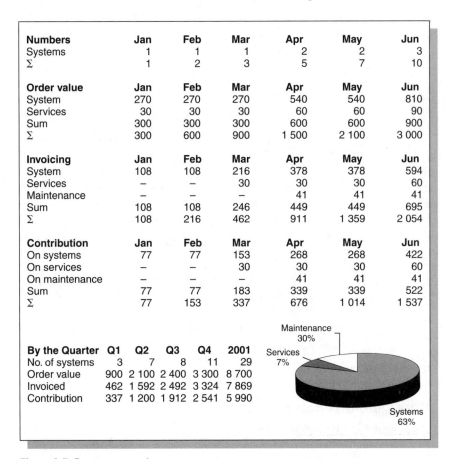

Numbers	Jan	Feb	Mar	Apr	May	Jun
Systems	1	1	1	2	2	3
Σ	1	2	3	5	7	10

Order value	Jan	Feb	Mar	Apr	May	Jun
System	270	270	270	540	540	810
Services	30	30	30	60	60	90
Sum	300	300	300	600	600	900
Σ	300	600	900	1 500	2 100	3 000

Invoicing	Jan	Feb	Mar	Apr	May	Jun
System	108	108	216	378	378	594
Services	–	–	30	30	30	60
Maintenance	–	–	–	41	41	41
Sum	108	108	246	449	449	695
Σ	108	216	462	911	1 359	2 054

Contribution	Jan	Feb	Mar	Apr	May	Jun
On systems	77	77	153	268	268	422
On services	–	–	30	30	30	60
On maintenance	–	–	–	41	41	41
Sum	77	77	183	339	339	522
Σ	77	153	337	676	1 014	1 537

By the Quarter	Q1	Q2	Q3	Q4	2001
No. of systems	3	7	8	11	29
Order value	900	2 100	2 400	3 300	8 700
Invoiced	462	1 592	2 492	3 324	7 869
Contribution	337	1 200	1 912	2 541	5 990

Maintenance 30%
Services 7%
Systems 63%

Figure 9.5 Forecast example

If you make a similar type of spreadsheet for the registration of the *actual* sales in volume and revenue, you have created yourself a handy tool for tracking the progress of your product.

Other options to consider:

- When parameters are not constant during the year, put them in the month column so that changes in pricing or margin can be easily entered.

- When adding the average time to collect bills, create a starting point for finance to make a cash flow overview.

The creation of the forecast is not something to do on your own. Although your knowledge of the market and your careful planning of the product strategy makes you an expert, you should consult other colleagues, like those responsible for sales, distribution and finance.

Conclusions

The product manager cannot produce a product plan, the business plan for his product, without the skills to do some basic financial calculations:

- The BEP, to be able to calculate the minimum volume of products to be sold to earn back the investments made. In other words, to break even.

- The ROI, to calculate how effective the investment in a product is.

- Cash flow calculations, based on sales and financial forecast, to be able to calculate the need for cash.

Although the finance department can help you making these calculations, it is important that you can make them yourself and understand them.

Interesting links on the web

Formulas for financial calculations

http://www.wheatworks.com/formula.htm

About the ROI

http://www.dmreview.com/article_sub.cfm?articleId=2487
http://www.jimnovo.com/ROI-Calculation.htm

About the forecast

http://www.marketingprofs.com/4/lapointe1.asp

You and the sales force

You can't live without 'em

Objectives

In many companies there is a friction between marketing and sales. But there should not be. The objective of this chapter is to give you instruments to work together with the sales people as one team, pursuing the same goal: To win.

If you compare a company with a soccer team, then the sales organization is like the center forward, the goal-getter. And in order for a center forward to score, he needs a lot of support from the rest of the team. The whole team needs to work together to maneuver the center forward into the right position. No match can be won without scoring. And there is no business without sales.

You as the product manager want your sales force to score with your product. Therefore you need to support them in every way possible.

This chapter looks at ways you can help your sales force score:

1 The sales kit. Helpful information and examples you can, or should, include in the sales kit on how to build a successful sales force are:
   - Product information
   - Sales presentation
   - Prospect information
   - Balanced scorecard
   - Competitive information

2 Sales visits and sales support

3 Filling the sales pipeline: lead generation

4 Bid support

The sales kit

Every company is different and every product needs a different type of sales kit. But there are some essentials that should be included in the content of every sales kit. All the information needed for the sales force has already been gathered by you during the product definition and the development of your strategy. It only needs a bit of reshuffling and to be put into another format.

Product information

What the sales force needs is all sales arguments and background information, to be used as ammunition during a sales pitch and to better inform the customer. The basis for this is already in your product plan, which is in fact a very interesting document for the sales force to read and have in their sales kit. It is certainly not a document to leave behind at the customer, but it gives the sales representative a lot of information about the product, its features and benefits, and the market you are targeting.

For peace of mind (both theirs and yours), the sales team needs to know about the strengths *and* weaknesses of the product. Yes, also the weaknesses. Every product has its weakness and it is very helpful to the sales force if you not only listed them, but also provided a 'how to' list of responses if a customer objects.

What they also need is an understanding of the delivery or installation process, as well as training possibilities, requirements and conditions. The partners that provide these services and what these services or additional products add to the solution your customer is seeking. In other words, the whole product.

In addition, they need to be able to name the USPs of your product, even when you wake them up in the middle of the night. Whenever possible, the USPs should be directly related to specific customer situations, issues and needs.

The sales kit should contain all sorts of the marketing materials the salesperson can leave behind. Brochures, white papers, data sheets, a self-running demo on CD, reprints of favorable articles or whatever you have created to promote your product (earlier described *materials needed* on p. 87). To be honest, marketing materials are not nearly as important as background information. The danger is that these materials often give sales people a false sense of confidence. The real confidence should come from their knowledge of the product and the customer. Remember, the customer seldom buys based on a brochure. The buying decision is primarily based on a 'good feeling' and a sense of trust from the sales representative.

The sales presentation

Another important item in the sales kit is the sales presentation. It is your script for the salesperson to help them highlight all the important information about your product and to position it the way you like. Even if the presentation slides are not used during the sales pitch, they should be in the mind of the sales representative when talking to the customer. Here are some tips for compiling sales presentations:

- Do not put too much information in a presentation. It is not a brochure! Decide what the main message is and concentrate on that main message throughout the presentation.

- The presentation is no more than a tool to support the story of the sales rep. It does not replace the story. Therefore, the slides should contain only keywords instead of whole sentences (let alone entire paragraphs) of text. Be sparse with anything that can distract from the story of your sales rep.

- In general, use a maximum of five bullet points per slide. Each bullet point should preferably contain just one to three words. Use a large, easy to read font type, so that the presentation can also be used with a larger group of people.

- Be sparse with the usage of animation effects. If you must, think about how it adds to your message. It is often too distracting, and the only message it sends is that you know how to use MS PowerPoint. Animation effects that the presenter has to wait for during the story will be irritating not only for the presenter, but also for the audience.

- Tell the salesperson what to say in the speaker notes. Give them real-life examples that can be used in their presentation and highlight the important points to get across.

- Make it easy for the salesperson to add their name and the prospect company's name and logo to the presentation (logos are almost always available on the Internet). In the speaker notes you can explain to a salesperson how to customize a presentation.

- Do not put a lot of background information about your company in the presentation. The primary interest of the prospect is the benefits of your product and what it can do for them.

- Try to limit the presentation to 10 slides. Each slide takes about two minutes and it is unlikely that your prospect can concentrate on what you or your sales rep wants to tell for longer than 20 minutes.

- Content wise, first get the attention of your prospect by picturing a recognizable issue or need, and then explain how your product is addressing them in a unique manner. Talk about the features and benefits (put the benefits on the slide and explain what feature results in this benefit), highlight the USPs and summarize how your product can improve their business. And then show the customer where to sign!

- It is not necessary to put everything you want to say in the exact words on the slides. Again, the slides are nothing more than a tool to support the story.

A slide just stating . . .

WOW!

. . . is often much more effective than a listing of all the benefits. It is up to you to make sure the sales reps tell the story the way you want them to. Tell them how, train them, help them and show them the way.

- The sales presentation is not an item to hand out (hard copy or soft copy) to the prospect. It should always be accompanied by the story. That is what self-running demos, brochures and websites are for.

Prospect information

The sales representative needs to learn as much as possible about the type of customer, the business of the customer, their daily issues and the jargon they use. The sales reps should do anything possible to provide the customer with that warm feeling that they know their business. The sales rep should act almost like a business partner. You should already have your ideal customer well profiled from the positioning exercise. The knowledge you have about the market segment and the prospect needs to be given prominent space in the sales kit.

The information about your target market and prospects is ever changing and newsworthy market information should be forwarded to the sales force. If your company has an intranet for publishing internal information, it can also be used to publicize URLs to informative e-zines and portals relevant to your target market segment.

The balanced scorecard

There should always be a way of assessing the advisability of spending much time in converting a prospect into a customer. The prospects the sales people should go after are those that come close to the ideal customer you have described in step 2 of the product positioning (Chapter 5). How well a prospect matches your ideal client can be graphically plotted in a so-called balanced scorecard. Including a 'balanced scorecard' in the sales kit can help both the sales people and you. It helps the sales people in not to waste time on prospects with the wrong profile and it helps in staying focused on the chosen target market. Perhaps you are already using a similar scoring system. Several useful software packages are available for this purpose, but at first assessment, the creation of your own tool is not that hard. If you are creating one for the first time, make sure it is easy to use. The sales rep cannot afford (and probably would not want) to spend a half-hour filling in all kinds of questions. For the first assessment, a simple Excel Spreadsheet can be used, with radio buttons for scoring and a radar graph for graphical representation of the scorecard as shown in Figure 10.1.

Enter your own questions in the balanced scorecard, categorize them, calculate the average score and place it on the axis of your choice. A balanced scorecard created in Excel takes less than five minutes to complete and gives a good indication of the attractiveness of the prospected client.

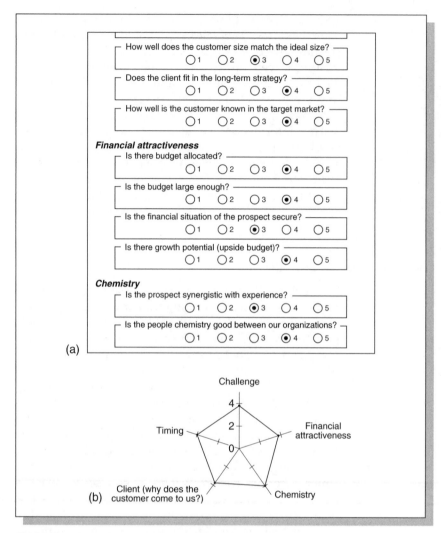

Figure 10.1 Balanced scorecard: (a) fill-in screen and (b) sample graph

Competitive information

A third section of the sales kit should be dedicated to competitive information and address these types of questions:

- Who are your main competitors?

- What are their strengths and weaknesses? How do you react to their strengths and what opportunities are offered by their weaknesses?

- What is their pricing policy and how does it relate to yours?

- What is the competitor's distribution strategy and what do you know about their channels and partners?

- How do they position themselves and their products and how does it compare to your positioning?

- Include URLs to the competitor's websites, so sales people can easily update themselves.

This can be published in hard copy or soft copy. But you might also consider entering all of this into an easy-to-maintain database. A CRM tool, if your company has one, is ideal to act as the central source for competitive information.

Sales visits and sales support

You are the one person in the company, who knows the product best. You understand both the technical and commercial aspects, you know the target market, as well as the vision, strategy and initial idea behind the product.

You can be of enormous help to the sales team. In my view, you are the ultimate expert and the owner of the product and should therefore offer your support in anyway possible, including going with them from time to time on sales visits or doing sales presentations at your office.

The benefits:

- You can help open doors that would otherwise remain closed and help to convince prospects.

- There is no better training for the sales rep than to see you at work, giving a sales presentation.

- The only way for you to get first-hand feedback from the market is by talking, and more importantly listening, to customers and prospects. This feedback can be used to further improve the sales presentation, positioning strategy, customer profiles and your own presentations.

Note Be cautious not to take the lead! The sales rep is the one in charge of the relationship. You have been brought in simply for your expertise on the product. So never ruin the authority of the sales rep.

Although you have many other tasks to do, and will not likely have enough time to meet every request for support, sales should not be pushed aside. Always take time to evaluate prospect presentations with the sales people. Estimate that you will spend as much as 20 percent of your time with the sales team.

Filling the sales pipeline: Lead generation

At the beginning of this chapter, the sales force was compared to the center forward of a soccer team. Bring your center forward into scoring position and try to give the perfect cross. It should not be just a meager shot somewhat in the direction of the goal-getter. Direction, length, timing, everything should be perfect. The same goes for the leads you hand to your sales team.

The essential goal of product promotion is to generate leads for the sales force. It is your job as product manager to help find those new leads, conduct pre-qualification assessments and hand those leads worth chasing over to the sales department.

A suspect is a potential customer

The process of getting suspects interested in your product and turning them into leads is often referred to as the sales pipeline or the sales funnel. If you take a look at the number of suspects, the initial contacts, compared to those that make it through the final stage, the process of selecting and sifting, though acting more as a filter, takes the shape of a funnel (Figure 10.2).

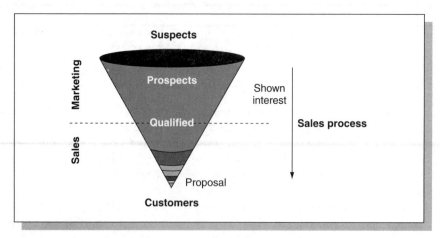

Figure 10.2 The sales funnel

The more you know about who those suspects are that are the most likely to make it to customer, the better the sales process works. It all goes back to positioning and narrowing your target market. Suspects are those companies or people that might be interested in your product. You have to reach them with your marketing campaigns and promotion. Because of your homework done, you know who they are and what triggers them. When a suspect shows interest in your product, it is called a prospect or a lead. The ratio between prospects and closed sales is called the conversion rate. For some products, the conversion rate is 100:1. For others it is closer to 10:1. Whatever the ratio is for your product in your market segment, do not bombard the sales force with unqualified prospects.

A quality lead is a prospect with a high conversion chance

Drawn as a process, the lead qualification will look like Figure 10.3.

In today's competitive climate, effectively managing the flow of quality leads through your sales process

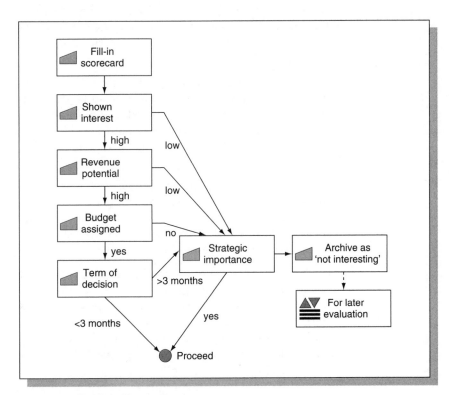

Figure 10.3 Lead qualification process

directly impacts the speed and rate of sales wins. Giving your sales force only the best prospects drives higher conversion of prospects to customers. Use your balanced scorecard or any other lead qualification method to not clog the sales pipeline with useless suspects.

The ratio between leads and customers is an important thing to keep track of. This tells you how many leads you have to generate in order to achieve the forecasted sales.

Carefully evaluate:

- The quality of the suspects and the leads. Are the suspects responding to your campaign the quality leads you want to have? Or is there a mismatch between the suspects you want to address and the ones actually responding? If so, something in your marketing message is off and you have to correct it!

- The ratios between suspects and leads and leads and customers. It gives you valuable indications of the workload you are generating for your sales force and the rest of the company. It tells you how many suspects you have to reach to generate the number of leads needed.

- The average time needed to convert a lead into a customer. This information is very important for planning campaigns and how campaigns affects your forecast, when this effect takes place or what the best time of the year you can start a marketing campaign.

- The sources suspects or leads are coming from. Following the sales pipeline, you will learn what marketing tools and media works best for your product. Is it advertising and if so, using what type of media? Are coupons successful? Make sure you know the source of your lead!

- Cost per lead and cost per customer. If your analysis of the sales process shows you that you need an average of 100 leads for every closed sale, then you know the value of a lead. You will know upfront how many leads are to be generated by a direct marketing campaign, an advertisement or any other marketing effort.

Today, there are many good CRM tools that provide excellent support in analyzing the sales pipeline.

Bid support

The more complex the product or service is, the more thoroughly constructed the proposal or bid should be. It is your job to help the sales rep in compiling a realistic bid for the prospect. This is particularly true for products that have many options, such as customization, installation, SI or training. If this is the case, you might consider setting up a 'bid team' to support the sales representative at an early stage.

A complaint often heard throughout the technology industry is that sales people are always overpromising. Perhaps they tell the customer the product will be installed within a time frame that can never be met. Or they sell a combination of features that is impossible to function with the hardware offered. Or they give the customer a discount that leaves no margin for profit.

If this sounds familiar, instead of blaming the sales people for overpromising, do something about it by becoming involved in the bid compilation process. With the help of a bid team, with representatives from each department involved, you can clearly define the boundaries of what sales can offer before bringing out a bid to the potential customer.

For the sales force, create a clear bid process that addresses the following issues:

1 Does the proposed bid comply with product standards? If any of the parameters – such as price, delivery/installation time, installation conditions, training, options or additional services – are not compliant, then it must be reviewed by the bid team.

2 What are the concerns of salesperson? Provide the sales rep with a simple list of questions. This saves time and forces the sales rep to think about his/her arguments.

3 What are the needs, wishes and circumstances of the prospect? The proposed bid should address each of these issues. Finally, present the proposal to the bid team for a final review.

Example: For a company delivering services involving installation of equipment and defined by a Service Level Agreement (SLA), a simple bid management process is shown in Figure 10.4.

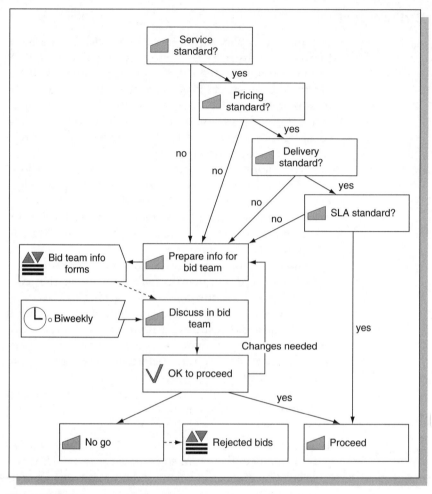

Figure 10.4 Bid management process

The advantages of installing a bid team are:

- No more complaints about the sales force. Involving other departments at an early stage of the sales process has a remarkable effect – it narrows the gap between the sales force and the rest of the company, creates understanding on both sides and stimulates teamwork. Sales becomes a combined responsibility and at the end a combined success.

- It helps the other departments with planning. Even before an order comes in, they know what to expect.

- In the event the bid needs to be re-constructed, the bid team functions as a think tank helping to come up with alternatives for the sales rep.

- When compiling the bid, the sales rep can ask for help from the experts at an early stage. Getting the support and back-up from the rest of the company gives the sales rep the essential confidence needed to successfully close the deal.

Conclusions

It is essential for the success of your product that you help the sales force as best as you can, by:

- Providing them all the information needed for their sales pitch in the sales kit, including product information (benefits!), competitive information and market information.

- Providing them with tools that can make the sales easier, such as a pricing tool.

- Giving them support and assistance with presentations, customer visits and bid support.

- Handing them qualified leads.

Interesting links on the web

About presentation skills

http://www.nwlink.com/~donclark/leader/leadpres.html
http://www.mapnp.org/library/commskls/presntng/basics.htm

About lead generation and qualification

http://www.powerhomebiz.com/vol22/leadqualification.htm
http://www.clickz.com/experts/archives/media/media_sell/article.php/820571

You and the engineers

Creating a balance between creativity and market needs

Objectives

In this chapter, the relationship with the development department is discussed and contains the following subjects:

1 How does the development process look like?

2 How can you stay in control over the product specifications, knowing that there will be changes to the functional specifications?

3 What is the difference between the alpha and beta stage in the development process?

4 How can you structure requests and ideas for next releases?

5 Suggestions for the creation of an 'improvement database'.

Most companies in the ICT sector start off as technology-driven. As explained in previous chapters, in order to achieve sustainable success, product development needs to be in line with market needs. But the goals of the product manager do not always match up with those of the engineering team. Pricing and time-to-market strategies can come into conflict with the natural strive for innovation and technical perfection. You often have to compromise on quality and feature-richness, which will not help you making you popular to the developers. This chapter provides the product manager with guidelines for the interaction with the development team.

The method on how to define and design a new product has been described earlier in Chapter 3. With the introduction of a product, there will be Requests for Changes (RFCs), bug fixes and improvements, caused by imperfections, technological developments, competition and the change in maturity of the market.

Your role as a product manager is a precarious one. You are not the chief technology officer (CTO) nor are you in charge of product development. Never forget that you are the virtual owner of the product the engineers are developing. Even though you are not in control of actual timelines or schedules, you will be held responsible for timely product introductions.

Unlike the situation with the sales force, you will never be able to provide the engineers with the kinds of tools and support that make their life easier. So what is the incentive for the engineering team to cooperate? The answer is simple; they are proud of what they create and they want their products, their babies, to be successful, also commercially. You can motivate them through inspiration, and you also can motivate them with good arguments. Engineers tend to be analytical and will therefore recognize a valid argument when they hear one. Team up with the engineers and establish a constructive two-way dialog.

Through this kind of interaction, you can make their lives easier by serving as both a communication channel and buffer between their department and the sales team.

One of the biggest challenges when dealing with the engineering team is staying in control of your product. Quite often, the development department makes its own decisions on implementation, such as when and how to fix bugs, create new functions, releases or product updates. I am not advocating that you patronize the developers by constantly looking over their shoulder, but to prevent surprises it is important to stay in close contact with the developers. Build in regularly scheduled time to discuss planning and any issues they are facing and the opportunities and challenges you see in the market and hear from the sales force.

It is important that you are not only informed of, but also involved in any of the following:

- Changes to the initial functional specs.

- Changes to planning.

- Functionality for next releases.

Changes to the initial functional specs

So let us say everyone has already agreed to the functional specifications and the product has been described in detail. In almost every case, the final product will look different than the original specs. When the engineers start developing, it is almost inevitable that they will encounter unforeseen problems and see new opportunities. They discover that one function will never work as described unless another is added or revised and so on. Specifications can be also interpreted in multiple ways when functions are not clearly described.

Even if there is nothing wrong with the product or the functional specifications, during the process of development, engineers will always have good suggestions and valid RFCs to the functional specifications. Do not try to stop or limit their creativity, as long as you are kept in the loop and are assured that at some point in development functional specifications can be 'frozen'. The point of freezing the functional specs marks the moment where creativity stops and where no more changes and additions are allowed.

Get to know and understand the working process of the development team. It will most likely have several stages, and when plotted out will look something like Figure 11.1.

What the (simplified) development process of Figure 11.1 represents are:

- The alpha-stage of the development process is the actual creation of the functionality. During this stage, engineers will come up with RFCs to the original

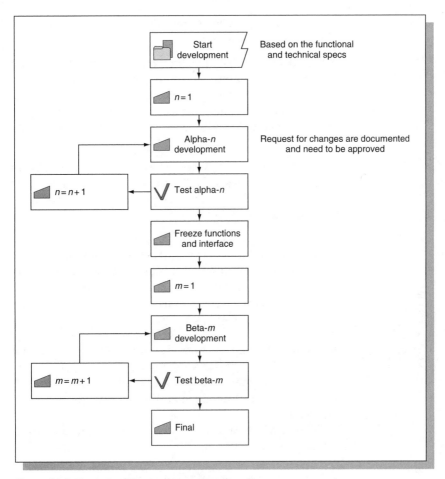

Figure 11.1 Example of the development process flow

design, both on function or feature level as to the design of the user interface. Any RFCs must first go through you, this can affect usability, and even price of the final product. Only RFCs that have been approved by you can be accepted.

- During the alpha stage, there is a lot of testing on how certain functions can be implemented, but at some point a decision must be made. At this point, development goes from alpha to beta stage. The specifications and the interface is frozen and the exact feature-set of the product and interface is set. Keep in mind that some of the original functions described will not make it into the final product, due to technical infeasibility or time-to-market constraints. Entering the beta-stage is an important milestone.

- The beta-stage of development is devoted to fixing bugs, documenting and finishing what was created during alpha development. Because the specifications and interface of the product are now fixed, the creation of user manuals, trainings and marketing materials can begin.

- The beta-stage of development is a good time to begin first customer tests. The early adaptors, or techies (see Figure 6.1), of your target segment can begin performing the necessary field tests.

- Successfully finishing beta testing does not necessarily mean that no more bugs will be found in your product or even that all known bugs are eliminated. Based on the amount of time you have, make the choice to accept certain imperfections, as long as the product does not contain any real 'show-stoppers'.

Reaching the end of beta development does still not mean you have a 'final' version of your product. It often takes several 'final candidates' to reach the final product. In software terminology this often is referred to as the Golden Master.

There are several documents required from the development team, including:

- List of known bugs or imperfections.

- Test reports, including test conditions.

- Full documentation on all implemented features.

Structuring of 'next releases'

No matter how well your product is designed and developed, it will never be perfect. There will always be faults and features that will not make it to the current release. During deployment of the product there will be requests and ideas for new features.

As the product manager, it is up to you to review those ideas for changes and improvements and decide which of them will be included in the new release of the product.

If you do not take the lead in managing the proposed changes to the product you risk losing control over the next release. Keep close track of all proposed changes as well as actual changes to the product and discuss them on a regular basis with the head of engineering.

This can be done using a simple text document or with a spreadsheet. The best method is a structured collection of ideas and bugs, maintained through the use of a database. An example is shown in Figure 11.2.

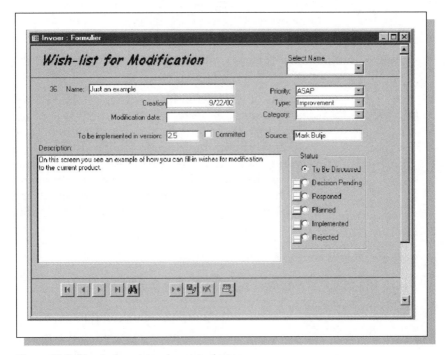

Figure 11.2 Structuring wishes for next releases

Here is a description showing some of the advantages to setting up a database:

- Figure 11.2 is the main input screen of a database created in MS Access.

- The *priority* field with a drop-down menu indicates the urgency of the desired change (like ASAP, High, Low, Medium).

- The *type* with a drop-down menu contains choices like 'Bug Fix', 'Addition' and 'Improvement'.

- The *Category* with a drop-down menu is used to categorize the wishes and contains selection choices such as 'SW functions', 'HW support', 'Interface', 'Integration', 'Documentation' and so on.

- The field 'to be implemented in version' contains requests for which release the feature should be implemented. The check box to the right of the field ('Committed') is checked when it is indeed no longer a wish, but a commitment for the release indicated. These two fields can be used to create a list of all commitments and a list of the wishes to discuss in your next meeting with the development team.

- The *Source* field contains the name of the person who generated this wish or request.

- The status of a record in the database can be selected using the radio buttons on the lower right side of the screen. This is the main selection criteria for periodical meetings with the developers. 'To be discussed' is everything new in the database. Any decisions made following that discussion can be selected afterward. On each decision, you can also add comments by clicking on the button to the left of the selected radio button as pictured below:

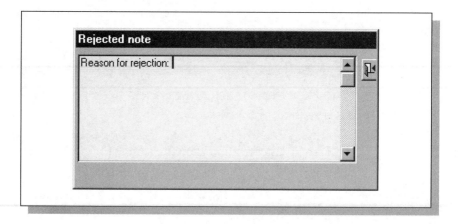

- Based on the database you have created, you can create reports for items to discuss, including new features and the fixing of bugs. You have now created yourself a structure for debating and managing the changes that will be implemented in new releases of existing products.

In addition to any regularly scheduled meetings with the development team about improvements to the product, it is important to share your goals for the product and any successes made on sales front. Involve them, ask their opinion and brainstorm on ways to benefit most from technological advantages and new developments.

Conclusions

Become the person who informs the rest of the company on the success and progress of the development team and act as the buffer between engineering and sales. Give engineering the credit and explain to everyone what these developments mean in terms of benefits and new opportunities.

The creativity of the engineers can and needs to be guided toward the development of a commercially viable product. You can do that with frequent and structured communication toward the engineering team and by acting as the interface between them and the sales force.

Interesting links on the web

http://www.cooper.com/content/insights/newsletters/2003_09/Features_talk_but_behaviors_close.asp

CHAPTER 12

If your product is a service

Going the extra mile

Objectives

The previous chapters did not distin-
guish services from 'normal' products;
the objective of this chapter is to have
a closer look at products, packaged
as services. What you will learn in this
chapter:

1 What extras you have to do in
  terms of defining and describing
  the service?

2 How to measure and control the
  performance of the service?

3 Some organizational aspects for
  service management.

If you are the product manager in a service-oriented company, you are not just delivering technology disguised as a product, you are providing that product as a service. So in addition to all of the steps described in this book, you will have to go that extra mile, and provide your customers with what is known as the SLA.

This chapter will give you an introduction to:

- The Service Level Agreement.

- Key Performance Indicators (KPIs) and KPI reporting.

- The importance of processes.

The Service Level Agreement

When you are selling a service, the most important benefit you are delivering to the customer is comfort. The comfort that you are taking over some of the customer's sorrows and the comfort that the customer does not have to worry about whatever it is that he trusts you to take care off. What it is that you are taking care of are the features/benefits of the service and can be treated as the features and benefits as any other product in the way described in the previous chapters. What you are providing with your service and how and when it is available to the customer is described in the SLA. Although every service is different, here are some general rules and tips for creating an SLA.

The principles of the SLA

- It should be customer focused and describe what the service brings to the customer, and how it helps them.

- It should describe the quality of service (QoS) the customer can expect.

- It sets expectations and allows the service become predictable.

- It should describe the conditions and agreements between the two parties.

The contents of the SLA should focus on the following:

- *Scope of the agreement*: This is a general overview of the SLA, in which the two parties are named and the length of the agreement is defined. Other issues such as general terms of conditions, disclaimers and references to laws should also be stated in this chapter.

- *The service definition*: This chapter should contain the description of the service provided. Systems used, databases or other (technical) details are less relevant than the functionality of the service. In many cases it is also wise to describe where the service will be used, by how many people and any limitations. Some companies prefer to add the whole service definition itself in an addendum to the SLA and make a reference from this chapter to the addendum or addenda. This is especially wise in case the SLA has to cover multiple services. In this chapter of the SLA you also state how (and if) the service and its features can change during the time of the agreement and how this will be communicated to the customer.

- *Definitions of terminology used*: This chapter needs to be inserted in the SLA to make sure that you and your customer have the same understanding on any terms used in the SLA. Clearly define, for example, what you define as a problem and what as an incident. Define what your 'window of service' is, how you calculate 'uptime' and 'downtime' of your service, define the difference between an update and an upgrade or anything that is applicable to your service and used in the agreement.

- *Support*: Describe the service hours for the service level or levels and describe any exceptions if applicable (like holidays). Also describe in detail what is and what is not included in 'support'.

- *The Quality of Service and how it is measured*: This chapter of the SLA defines clearly when the service is available for usage by the customer and to what extent or at what minimum performance level. Here you can also specify normal operating hours, special operating hours, exceptions, and how (and if) the time at which the service is used affects the performance of the service. Clearly specify how you are going to measure the QoS. In this chapter, you also describe when (and if) there are scheduled timeframes during which the service will not be available (for maintenance or back-up or whatever reason there is) for planned service interruptions.

- *The conditions under which you can guarantee the QoS*: What are the conditions the customer has to commit to in order to enable you to comply with the QoS promised? These conditions can range from external system requirements, like temperature, humidity, power supply and so on, to the skills of the users using your service. In this chapter you can also describe the access you need to install equipment and what you expect from them in case of a problem or incident.

- *The reporting you do on the service and its QoS*: In this chapter of the SLA you state how you will report on the usage of the service and on the metrics as defined in the QoS. Further, you can mention the frequency of the reporting and the medium or media (paper, CD-ROM, Internet) used to get the report(s) to the customer. If applicable, you can describe what extra reporting options you have available and at what price.

- *Dependencies on external services*: If your service includes or is depended on services from external parties, it should be clearly stated in the SLA and what the consequences of these dependencies are. For instance, if your service makes use of some connection for data communication, it will most likely use infrastructure from an external party. The availability and QoS of your service is dependent on the QoS and availability of the infrastructure provided by the third party. The consequences and/or disclaimers can be described here.

- *How and when to trigger action*? This chapter is almost a handbook on how to act in case of questions, need for support, incidents and problems and changes in the usage of the service. The latter could contain instructions in case the number of users changes, what to do to activate or deactivate features and functions, organizational changes and upgrade or downgrade to another service level.

- *How to handle disputes*? Of course you do not expect to have any disputes with your customer, but reality is that it sometimes happens. For both you and the customer, it is beneficial to explain what will be done in the case of a dispute. Is there an independent party with a final say in case of a dispute? What are the circumstances under which the agreement can be terminated (from either side)?

- *Organizational information*: Prime contact persons on both sides, names, responsibilities, telephone numbers and email addresses of account managers, support personnel, helpdesk, billing and collecting or any other organizational information relevant to your service can be specified here.

KPIs and KPI reporting

For a service organization, QoS is everything. To measure the QoS and to be able to steer on quality, the KPIs need to be defined.

The KPIs serve two major goals:

1 Measuring the performance of your company and service, in order to constantly improve the quality and steer on quality.

2 Have the performance indicators in metrics to show your customers how well your service is doing.

Because of these two goals, you will need KPIs for internal usage and others for external usage.

The definition of what the KPIs are for your product and your company depend to a large extent on the image you want to build for your product. For instance, if you position yourself as 'the most responsive', then make sure you have the KPIs to prove it or to steer on responsiveness:

- What is the average amount of rings before your customer service department picks up the phone? And what is the maximum? Is the maximum number still within acceptable limits?

- What is the average response time on emails? What is the maximum response time? What is the percentage of emails that was answered within the boundaries set?

- How long does it take to respond to a request for information? And so on.

Your set of KPIs are to a large extent different when you position your service as the most reliable. In that case you want to report on the up-time of the service, the number of successful transaction and their percentages, statistics on repair-time and problem-tickets.

The reports you generate with all the statistics should be color coded to highlight the exceptions. It is your control and steering mechanism to evaluate and improve the quality of your service.

Your internal reporting shows all the statistics for all customers, while you can decide to send your customer the statistics for their service – of course in line with what you agreed with your customer in the SLA.

Before defining the KPIs you want to report on, you have to carefully think about what can and should be done in case one or more of the figures are out of their pre-set boundaries. And what are these boundaries? The statistics are utterly useless if it does not trigger action at some point. So, after defining the KPIs you have to:

- Define the boundaries – the thresholds. These are the criteria to which a KPI is compared with. As soon a threshold is breached, the report can raise a flag 'look at me! Something is potentially wrong here'. Do set thresholds that give you some margin and warn you that a certain value is coming dangerously close to the minimum quality level agreed upon in the SLA. It then allows you to take measures in time.

  Example: Your SLA states that calls made to the helpdesk will be answered within five seconds in at least 80 percent of the incoming calls. You have defined one of your KPIs as 'the percentage of calls that is answered within five seconds'. You should set two thresholds: Of course a threshold at 80 percent, setting a 'red-code' alarm when the KPI drops below it, but you should also set an 'amber' alarm at for instance 88 percent, for this comes dangerously close to the minimum level.

- Define what needs to be done in case thresholds have been breached. What are the options you have when an 'amber' alarm is set? Do you just send out an email to the people at the helpdesk, urging them to pick up the phone sooner; do you just signal it to the helpdesk manager? Will it be an agenda point in the next KPI-meeting, where the QoS is discussed? And what to do in case of a 'red' alarm? Does the SLA state that you have to inform the customer? Are there penalties connected to it?

If a KPI does not call for action at some point, it is useless reporting on it. It is just one of the reasons why well-defined processes are an absolute must for every service provider.

The importance of processes

Predictability and a consistent level of service quality are essential to the success of the service organization. Predictability can be reached by lining out the processes for the organization. The processes around a service are, for the service, as important as the feature and function set – maybe even more important.

A process is a repeatable, connected series of actions. By describing these actions and putting them together in a process model, the predictability of the outcome is secured. Every process has a pre-defined goal and by comparing the results, the output of the process with the pre-defined goals, the process can be evaluated and improved if necessary.

Having well-defined processes makes your company less dependent on individuals. No customer will accept a disclaimer in your SLA where you state that the quality of the service can only be guaranteed as long as Mr So-and-so is still working for you. Processes share knowledge about how to do things, where to find the right type of information, who is responsible for what type of action or decision, what the criteria are to base decisions on and so on.

Processes are needed to describe:

- How the service is maintained, including processes for problem management, incident management and change management?

- How and when the service is installed?

- How and when the service is billed?

- How to act in case KPI thresholds are breached?

- How to handle customer request for support, helpdesk inquiries and customer complaints?

- Any other repeatable chain of actions required for your service.

When you describe the processes for your service, it is highly recommended to use a tool that not only uses paper, but that produces output in html format. Such a tool enables you to create an interactive process model on your intranet site, accessible for everybody. It has big advantages over 'just' a paper version of your processes:

- It is easy to maintain. A paper version tends to end up in binders all over the company and it is never clear whether the version in your binder is the latest one. A web-based version is centralized and can thus be always up-to-date, or at least everybody is using the same version.

- An interactive version of the processes can contain hyperlinks to templates and documents that are used during the process. It makes it far more encouraging to use the processes, and the documents and templates attached to it increase the uniformity and predictability.

- Browsing through the processes makes it easy for the users to quickly find their part of the process.

Conclusions

If your product is a service you need to carefully define to the customer what the service does and does not contain and how it is delivered to the customer. This is described in the SLA. To be able to report and steer on the quality and performance of the service, KPIs are defined, measured and reported on a regular basis.

For services and service-oriented companies, well-defined processes are essential to make the services repeatable, predictable, efficient and manageable. Processes are valuable marketing instruments for services.

Interesting links on the web

About SLAs

http://www.unisa.edu.au/quality/RSA/RSAhomepage.htm
http://www.remedy.com/solutions/documents/white_papers/Service_Level_Mgmt.pdf
http://www.nextslm.org/itilhelpdesk.html

About KPIs

http://www.nextslm.org/itilhelpdesk.html
http://management.about.com/cs/generalmanagement/a/keyperfindic.htm
http://directory.service.com/k/kpi.service.com.htm

CHAPTER 13

Managing the product portfolio

About cash cows, stars and dogs

Objectives

The objective of this final chapter is to provide you as the product manager with the information and methodologies needed to manage a portfolio of products.

You will learn about:

1 The Boston Consulting Group growth/share matrix.

2 The nine cells of General Electric/ McKinsey.

3 Pitfalls to avoid when marketing multiple products.

So far we have been talking about managing a single product and only briefly touched the fit of the product to the company's product portfolio. But unless you are product manager for a one-product company, you will have to carefully manage the company's product portfolio or the products belonging to one and the same product line.

This chapter looks at managing your product portfolio in order to

- Balance the cash flow.

- Optimize sales and revenue for the product line or company as a whole.

- Optimize marketing planning.

Managing your portfolio from a cash-flow perspective

Let us go back to the product life cycle (see Figure 1.1), but this time we add an extra line to it, showing the cash flow during the lifetime of the product.

The graphical representation of the cash flow in Figure 13.1 shows clearly how the product drains cash before it starts paying back and how the cash flow remains negative for quite a while even after introduction. This is caused by the efforts you have to take to fight for market share in an already existing market. In the beginning of the product life cycle you will spend

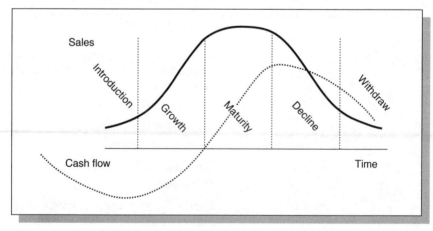

Figure 13.1 Cash flow related to the product life cycle

more money on marketing than the sales of the product will generate. By planning the product life cycles of your mix of products you can avoid hefty pressure on your cash position and you can subsidize the introduction and growth phase of one product by the positive cash flow of product that are more advanced in their life cycle (Figure 13.2).

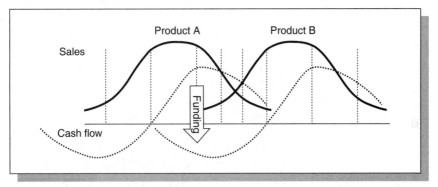

Figure 13.2 Product A funding Product B

This principle has been described and visualized in a widely used and very useful method for managing the company product portfolio by the Boston Consulting Group (BCG). In their method, they categorize products along two axes:

1 Market share

2 Market growth.

The parameter market share is important for indicating if a relatively large amount of money needs to be invested to increase market share. Building market share is expensive. The product life cycle shows the volume or revenue of the products sold, but it does not show whether the product at the top of the product life cycle curve gained enough market share to generate more cash than needed to market the product.

The second parameter, market growth, tells you something about the attractiveness or at least about the potential of the market. Introducing a product in a market with substantial growth is worth investing in, while there is no room for growth it justifies just harvesting what you have seeded or withdrawing from the market.

The BCG shows the market growth on the horizontal axis (x). BCG sets the range from 0 to 20 percent growth. This is rather arbitrary, but seems to work quite nicely in practice. The range itself is less important as the division between 'high' and 'low' market growth, which is set at 10 percent in the original BCG diagram.

The relative market share is shown on the vertical axis (y). The definition of relative market share is: the revenue compared to the largest competitor. In the original BCG growth/share matrix a scale was used from 0.1x to 10x. Market leadership is reached when the relative market share is above 1x and in the BCG matrix a relative market share above 1x is considered as 'high', everything below 1x is 'low'. Again, these choices are arbitrary and we will look at alternatives later.

The division of both axis in 'high' and 'low' creates four quadrants as shown in Figure 13.3.

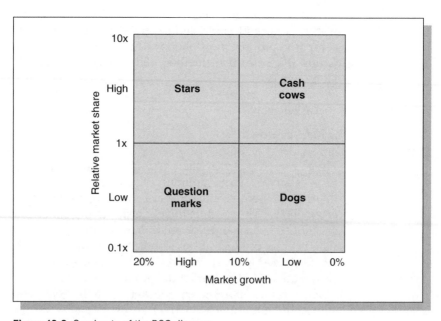

Figure 13.3 Quadrants of the BCG diagram

Question marks Products with a low relative market share in a market with a high growth rate.

- A low relative market share implies that there are established competitors in this market.
- A high growth rate of the market is an important indicator that the market is attractive.
- Your product is a small player in a fast growing market. To be successful, you have to gain market share and fight against the more dominant competitors. This is expensive and will result in a large negative cash flow.

At the beginning of a product life cycle, your product most likely starts as a question mark.

Stars Products with a high relative market share in a fast growing market.

- A high relative market share indicates high sales revenues and is the basis for long-term profitability.
- A high growth rate of the market demands continuous investments to keep up with the growth.
- Your product is a big player in a fast growing market. The rapid market growth is the result of a lot of activity in the market and the presence of heavy competition. Your product is a success in terms of revenue, but most of the revenue needs to be reinvested in marketing campaigns, market development, expending sales channels and other growth strategies to secure your leading position.

A successful question mark can reach market leadership and become a star: a market leader in high growth industries. Defending the position as the market leader and financing the growth often causes the star to be only marginally profitable.

Typically, in the product life cycle of the product, this is the growth phase targeting at the early adaptors. But as the market growth slows down and the product becomes more mature, the need for investments decreases and the profitability increases.

Cash cows   Products with a high relative market share in a low growth market.

- Market leadership equals high revenues.

- A low growth rate of the market does not require high investments.

- Your cash cow product has a comfortable leading position. Because of the low growth of the market, keeping your position as the market leader requires far less investments than needed for the star product.

The cash cow is, like the name indicates, the cash generator. Revenues are high, investments are low, so the cash cow generates a healthy positive cash flow. This is normally the 'maturity' phase of the product in its product life cycle. It is desirable to keep this position as long as possible.

Dogs   Products with a low relative market share in a market with low growth rate.

- The low relative market share causes poor revenues.

- The low growth rate of the market makes this market unattractive.

- Your product might be profitable, but does not generate much positive cash flow. The product is not a market leader and although it might be possible to increase market share, the low market growth rate does not make it very interesting to invest too much in this product.

If a cash cow loses market share, it becomes a dog and the product is most likely in last phase of the product life cycle, the decline.

Figure 13.4 shows the BCG's growth/share matrix with the optimum cash flow and product life cycle.

The product manager needs to manage his products in such a way that the cash cows of the portfolio generate more cash than the question marks consume, in order to be profitable. New question marks and stars are needed to be able to take over cash cow positions in the longer run. It is inevitable, certainly in the technology industry, that cash cows will lose market share and become dogs. In other words, there needs to be a good balance between the products.

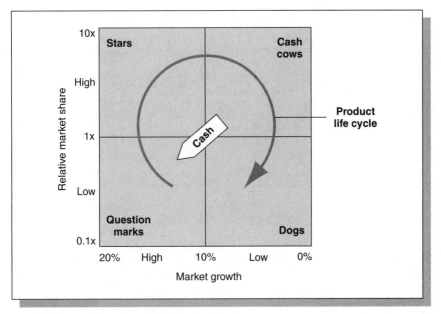

Figure 13.4 BCG's matrix with optimum PLC

Analyzing the product portfolio using BCG's matrix

The analysis of the portfolio starts with plotting all products as circles or balls in the growth/share matrix. With the size of the circle you can indicate the absolute revenue value of the product.

Let us take a look at a couple of examples.

The little arrows in Figure 13.5 indicate the trend. For instance, product 2 is positioned in a high growth market and is gaining market share and is likely to soon become a star.

Some of the conclusions you might draw about the product portfolio as drawn in Figure 13.5:

- *Overall picture*: not really out of balance although there are no real stars at the moment. Having no dogs in the portfolio is of course not a problem.

- *Product 1 is a question mark*: Market growth is not very high, but speeding up. The market share is still very low but improving. The path that product 1 seems to follow gives no reason for worry. A possible problem though is that product 1 is the only question mark in the portfolio. The market development for this product

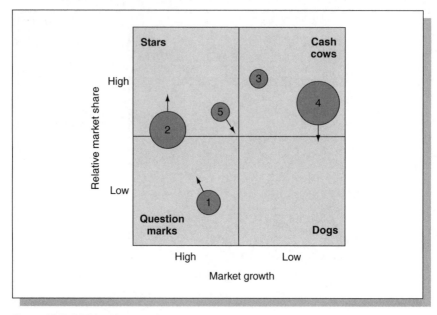

Figure 13.5 BCG matrix example 1

and the campaigns to increase its market share does not allow any mistakes.

- *Product 2 seems to grow into a real star*: The size of the circle indicates that the revenue generated is rather high, so the market this product is operating in must be big. We can also see that the market growth for product 2 is really high, so financing the growth of this product and increasing its market share most likely require even more cash at this stage. Product 2 seems to be promising.

- *Product 3 is not generating a lot of revenue*: But it is positioned at a (for a cash cow) nice position – market leadership in a low to moderate growing market. It seems to be stable and the strategy for this product should just be to consolidate.

- *The big cash cow in this portfolio is product 4*: Figure 13.5 also indicates that this product is losing its market share. This is a dangerous situation. The size of the circle is large but if the product is losing market share in a market that is hardly growing, the cash generated by product 4 is rapidly decreasing. To avoid that product 4 becomes a dog before any of the stars can take over the cash generating role, the strategy for product 4 should be focused on stabilizing market share. This could be done by product diversification, lowering price or promotional bundles with other products or services.

- *Product 5 is in a dangerous path*: It is losing market share in a growing market. It seems to be heading toward dog status before it has a chance to become a cash cow. If that happens the product will, measured over the whole lifetime of the product, not be profitable. The future possibilities for product 5 need to be carefully assessed to decide what strategy should be followed: investing extra money to revitalize the product or divest and withdraw the product from the market. Revitalization of the product is of course preferable and the product positioning and pricing need to be evaluated in light of the current competitive landscape.

If your product portfolio looks like Figure 13.6, it is quite clear that it is out of balance. The problem is that if you do not take the effort to plot it out like this, you will most likely be very satisfied with your portfolio and not

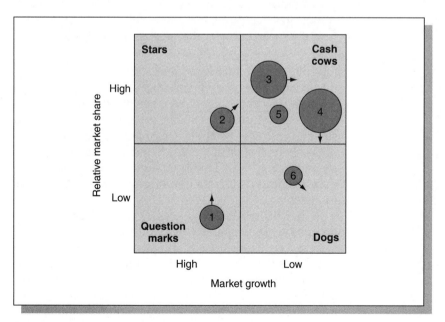

Figure 13.6 BCG matrix example 2

notice the dangerous situation that lies ahead of you. The portfolio shows three nice cash cows, so the company will not complain about the profitability.

- Product 1 is a question mark. You will not have any problems financing the development and marketing of this product. It is risky though to have only one question mark and the market product 1 operating shows high growth, but not a very high growth. The potential revenue of product 1 is uncertain.

- Product 2 is a star, but apparently the market is slowing down. The advantage of it is that the need to invest in product 2 is decreasing and it will become a cash cow pretty soon. The problem with a slowing down of market growth is that the potential revenue for product 2 is limited and there are already cash cows enough.

- The market share for product 3 and 5 remains stable so these products will likely continue to generate a positive cash flow in the near future.

- Product 4 is not doing well. Losing market share in a hardly growing market is not a good sign and without a strategy to increase market share of product 4 again, this product will soon be a dog. The size of the circle indicates that product is responsible for a hefty portion of the cash flow and that portion is in serious danger.

Overall, the products are competing in, from a growth rate perspective, not very attractive markets. Although the cash flow at present is very healthy, the mid to longer term does not provide enough products to take over the star and cash cow position of the current portfolio.

This is typical of the case when technology companies are not attentive or flexible enough to change and introduce new products in the rapid growing markets of that moment.

In the 1980s, WANG computers was a very successful and profitable company. Their word processing and office systems were positioned in high growth market. The strong position they took with their star products like the WANG OIS office system (word processing) and to a lesser extent the WANG VS mini-computer were financed by earlier stars and at that point cash cows like the WANG 2200 mini computer and the technical calculators before that. But new markets developed, like the market for PCs and cheap word processors and the growth of mini-computers and office systems came to an almost standstill. The WANG OIS and VS became powerful cash cows, but there were no real rising stars to secure WANG's position in the long run. The company became ignorant of the developments in the market, caused by the wonderful profits the company made on these products and the seemingly untouchable leadership. When the company recognized that their OIS and VS systems were rapidly losing market share to the new (competing) stars, like Word Perfect for word processing, WANG tried to introduce new products. They developed an image processing computer and a database engine (PACE) for their VS mini-computer in an attempt to enter new, attractive market segments. These were both great products from a technical point of view, but the necessary product and market development could not be financed, for their cash cows became dogs.

The example of a product portfolio in Figure 13.7 has one major problem: There are many stars and question marks, but only one cash cow. And the trends, indicated by the small arrows are very alarming indeed. The stars of today do not seem to make it to the status of cash

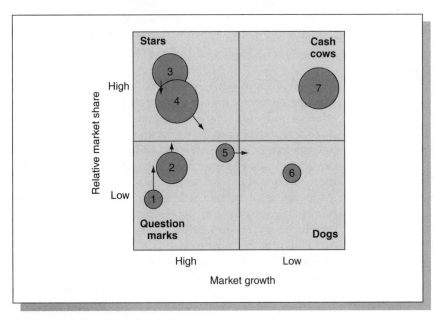

Figure 13.7 BCG matrix example 3

cow. Product 4 is losing market share in a shrinking market. Product 3 is losing market share to the competition in a still attractive (at least healthy growing) market. What could be the explanation for such a dramatic development?

- One explanation could be that the company (the product manager!) is paying too much attention to the new products of the portfolio, the question marks. In Figure 13.7 we see three question marks, probably all newly introduced products. Most of the attention goes to the development and introduction of new products, prohibiting the rising stars to grow to full maturity. All marketing money is thrown at the newcomers, while the stars ready to generate the badly needed cash are ignored.

- A second explanation, often in combination with the one described, is the effect of cannibalization. If products 1 and 2 in Figure 13.7 are targeted at the same market as products 3 and 4, with most likely even better features, then they are gaining market only at the cost of the stars, and the stars will quickly lose market share and become obsolete. In other words, products 1 and 2 are introduced too early or products 3 and 4 should not have been introduced at the first place. Waiting for the introduction of products 1 and 2 would have been a lot less expensive.

The BCG's growth/share matrix of Figure 13.7 is unfortunately symptomatic for many companies in the IT and telecom industry. The time-to-market dogma rules are often misunderstood. Many technology companies seem to think that cranking out new products at the fastest pace possible is the most important thing. Time to market is far more important though, as is attention to marketing.

Operators of mobile telephony networks around the world are introducing new services, based on newly developed techniques, while the currently used technology is hardly (if even) paid for. In other words, stars are moving in the direction of dogs, skipping the cash cow phase. GSM, the 'second generation' (or 2G) of mobile telephony, is still a star in 2000 and 2001 when hefty investments (over $45 billion) are made in UMTS (3G), auctioned by European governments. The first UMTS services were expected to be introduced in 2002, but at the time of publication of this book (2004) only NTT DoCoMo in Japan would have commercially launched UMTS services, while UMTS revenue forecast in Western Europe for 2005 is less then 3 percent of total mobile service revenues. The reason for the delay is not related to technology, but is purely economical. The operators needed to recover from the investments made for the acquisition of the UMTS licenses. A too early introduction of UMTS services and phones would have prevented the successful GSM technology to become a true cash cow.

The BCG's growth/share matrix is a useful method to plot the product portfolio of a company, a business unit or a product line and analyze strategies for investments and planning. It focuses on the cash flow and the balance between cash generators and cash spenders.

A balanced portfolio is essential because:

- Too many stars may lead to a cash crisis.

- Too many Cash Cows may put future profitability at risk.

- And too many question marks may affect current profitability.

But the method also has limitations.

Limitations of the BCG's growth/share matrix

The beauty of the BCG growth/share matrix is immediately its limitation: its simplicity. The usage of just two variables makes it very easy to use. But the argument that market attractiveness is not the same as market growth is defendable. And why is the division of 'high' and 'low' market share set at market leadership and the division between high and low market growth rate set at 10 percent? These choices are at least arbitrary. In short:

- Definition (qualitative and quantitative) of the market is sometimes difficult.

- It assumes that market share and profitability are directly related.

- The use of high and low to form four categories is too simplistic.

- Growth rate is only one aspect of industry attractiveness and high growth markets are not always the most profitable.

- It considers the product or business in relation to the largest player only. It ignores the impact of small competitors whose market share is rising fast.

- Market share is only one aspect of overall competitive position.

- It ignores interdependence and synergy.

Maybe the one biggest drawback of the BCG growth/share matrix is the relative market share, in which the competitive position is measured against the biggest player in the market. The industry of IT and Telecommunications is complex and very competitive. The difference between a question mark and a star in a fast growing market (or otherwise attractive market) is described well by Geoffrey Moore in his book *Crossing the Chasm*, in which he states that the minimum market share to 'cross the chasm' is 15 percent. So this is not related to or measured against the largest player in the market, but looks at the market as a whole.

For plotting the product portfolio of ICT products in a BCG's growth/share matrix, I found replacing the relative market share axis by a market share axis, where the barrier between 'high' and 'low' is at 15 percent.

The nine-cell matrix of General Electric/McKinsey

The method for portfolio management developed by General Electric and McKinsey shows a lot of similarities to the method of the BCG. As with the BCG, it comprises a matrix of two dimensions:

1 Market attractiveness

2 Competitive position or business strength.

These two dimensions, though are a lot more complex, for the values on both axes are composed of multiple variables to assess the market attractiveness and the competitive position in that market.

Market attractiveness can and will be a composition of variables that vary from company to company, but will most likely at least contain:

- Market growth rate
- Industry profitability
- Market size
- Vulnerability.

The value for business strength is not looking at the market itself, but at the position your product has in that market. It will be calculated using several variables, like:

- Profitability
- Technological position
- Market share
- Uniqueness.

Individual products are plotted as circles as shown in Figure 13.8. The area of the circles is proportional to the

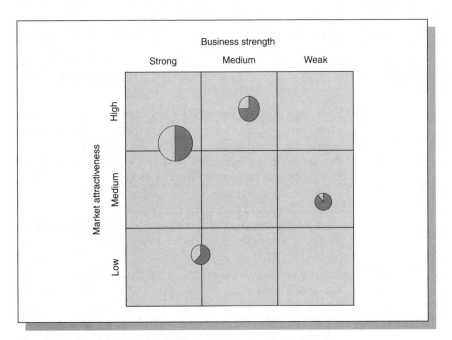

Figure 13.8 The GE/McKinsey matrix

industry size (in term of sales). The shaded pie represents the market share for each product.

The variables on both axes are to be defined by you. When you created the list of criteria relevant to your product and to the market you are operating in, you have to give each of the variables a weighting factor. Now you can assess the value of each criterion, rating it from 1 (not attractive at all) to 5 (very attractive). For each and every product you can calculate their compound value for the market attractiveness and for the competitive position/ business strength, like the example given in the table below for the assessment of the market attractiveness:

Attractiveness criteria	Weight	Rating	Weighted
Size	4	2	8
Growth	4	3	12
Profitability of the industry	4	4	16
Competitiveness	2	4	8
Stability/vulnerability	2	2	4
Customer budgets	2	4	8
			56
		Maximum:	90
		Score:	62%

Be aware to give rates from an attractiveness point of view. For instance, the market attractiveness is higher when the competitiveness is lower. The rate of '4' in the table above indicates that the market is attractive from a competitiveness point of view.

The score is the sum of the weighted ratings, divided by the maximum sum of ratings possible.

In a similar way, the score for competitive position or business strength is calculated. Products can now be plotted in the diagram. Note that the GE/McKinsey nine-cell matrix represents the external factors (the market attractiveness) along one axis and the internal factors (the business strength and competitive position) along the other axis. That is why this diagram is also often referred to as the internal–external matrix.

The GE/McKinsey matrix is divided into nine cells, instead of the four quadrants of the BCG matrix. Both the axes are divided into three segments. The market attractiveness axis is divided into high, medium and low and the business strength axis is divided into strong, medium and weak.

The products are represented as little pie charts, where the size of the pie chart indicates the size of the market and the wedge in the pie chart shows the market share of the product compared to the total market size.

An internal–external product portfolio analysis is shown in Figure 13.8.

As with the BCG matrix, the position of the product in Figure 13.8 is an indication of how well your portfolio is balanced and it gives important hints for strategy development. A strong product in an attractive market is a winner (equivalent to the star in the BCG matrix) and a strong product in a market with low attractiveness is a profit maker, the equivalence of the cash cow in the matrix of the BCG.

In the Figure 13.9, you find the qualifications for the products for each of the nine cells, along with the suggested strategy.

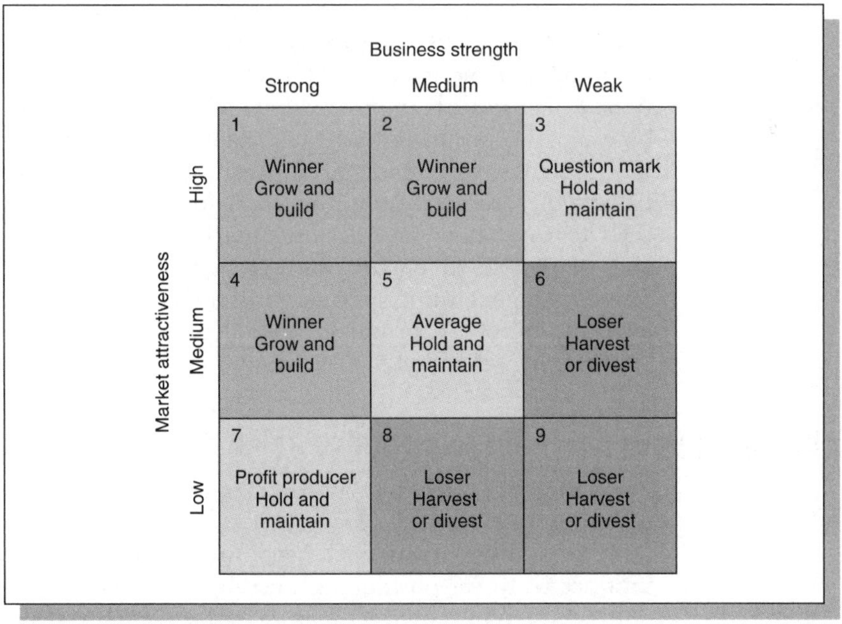

| | Business strength | | |
	Strong	Medium	Weak
High	1 Winner Grow and build	2 Winner Grow and build	3 Question mark Hold and maintain
Medium	4 Winner Grow and build	5 Average Hold and maintain	6 Loser Harvest or divest
Low	7 Profit producer Hold and maintain	8 Loser Harvest or divest	9 Loser Harvest or divest

(Market attractiveness)

Figure 13.9 The nine cells of GE/McKinsey

The nine cells in the matrix can be divided into three strategy groups:

1 For cells 1, 2 and 4, the appropriate strategies might be *Grow and build*. The market in which the product is operating is relatively strong and so is the business strength for that particular product.

2 The prescription for cells 3, 5 and 7 is likely to be *Hold and maintain*.

3 Finally, cells 6, 8 and 9, which are characterized by a relatively weak competitive position in a hostile environment, would suggest the appropriate strategies are either *Harvest* or *Divest*.

Successful companies will make an effort to build a portfolio of products in or around cell 1 in the IE matrix.

The GE/McKinsey matrix requires more information than the BCG's growth/share matrix and is felt to be a more thorough technique. But it is also much more dependant on your value judgments, the selection of criteria and the weight factors you assign to these criteria.

The methods of both the BCG and GE/McKinsey give you as the product manager good tips for strategy and planning by looking at the external market and the position of the products in that external market. The balance between the products and their stages in the product life cycle is important. The Cash Cows or Profit Generators are extremely important for generating the cash to fund new product and market developments and of course to ensure the company's profitability. These cash generating products will not survive forever and the follow-up products need to be ready to take over this lead position.

Managing your portfolio to optimize sales revenues

Managing your product portfolio and balancing and planning their life cycles are not only needed from a cash flow perspective; you also need to carefully balance product features, positioning and pricing between the products in your product line in order to achieve the optimum sales revenue and product line profits.

Here are some pitfalls to avoid:

- Cannibalization of other products.
- Contradicting messages.
- Too less product diversification.
- Too much product diversification.

Cannibalization of other products

Cranking out new products is both essential and danger-ous in the fast paced market of technology products. Without new products or releases of products to replace the current ones, you will not be able to stay ahead of the competition. But try not to become your own competitor.

When introducing, for example, a product for the low end of the market as an addition to your more profes-sional version, make sure it is really less functional than the higher priced product. If not, you are not just reach-ing an extra group of customers, but your existing cus-tomers are buying the cheaper product, thus lowering overall revenue.

The positioning of your product and the product line is your key instrument to differentiate products in the same product line enough to avoid cannibalization. Sales revenue can be optimized by stimulating up-selling to more feature-rich, more expensive products.

Contradicting messages

Be very careful not to confuse the market by sending out contradicting messages. When you introduce a new prod-uct to the market, make sure that your main message, your positioning of your new product is not ruining the positioning of an existing product. In many cases, you have to review the positioning of other products in your portfolio to reflect the new situation created by the newly introduced product.

A vendor of printers cannot promote color laser print-ers, saying that these printers are the top-of-the-line printers for professional usage and the same time pro-mote their inkjet printers, claiming photo-quality output of the best quality possible. It is contradicting and can-not be understood by the target audience.

Too less product diversification

People want the possibility to choose. A line of products, with an entry-level 'budget' version with just the bare minimum of functionality, a midrange version and a 'deluxe' high-end product gives the customer options to choose. On the top of that, it gives you better opportunities to market your product. Depending on the product you are marketing, you can also create modular products: core functionality in the base configuration, with optional features.

If you are targeting your product at several market segments, it is unlikely that the same product will excel in all of these market segments. The 'whole product', as discussed in Chapter 5, should be different to best accommodate the needs of that specific market. Although the core functionality might be the same, the complementary services and products are likely to be different.

Trying to create a 'one-size-fits-all' product is not a good idea.

Too much product diversification

Offering a large range of products, options and configurations, targeted at the same market segment, creates unnecessary complexity and will scare people off. If the customers cannot understand the difference between the products presented, or needs too much time to figure out what options will offer the best benefits to their situation, they are likely to go for the competing product they do understand.

The positioning of a product in comparison with other products in the product portfolio is almost as important as the positioning toward the customer, the external positioning. Each product needs its own micro-positioning reflected by the pricing, features, packaging, distribution and promotion. If you have a hard time explaining the differences between the products in your portfolio, or explaining the customer what product or feature to choose, then the customer will certainly be confused.

In case you want to buy a Dell laptop computer, it certainly is not 'as easy as Dell'. There are (summer 2004) no less than 15 models in three notebook product lines

(Inspiron Notebook, Lattitude Notebook and Precision Mobile Workstation). Each of these notebooks are available with different processors, processor speeds and monitor configurations plus an impressive list of other configuration choices. Counting only processor speed + monitor as separate configurations, the variance of Dell notebook computers mounts up to 107 (!). This does not seem to help the customer to make a choice. Although there is no proof (yet) that this actually harms Dell as a company, there are some alarming precedents. In the mid-1990s, Apple computer had a hard time explaining its prospective customers the difference between all the different Performas, Power Macs, Centrises and Quadras. Each of these products represented an average of 50 different models. The first task Steve Jobs undertook after returning to Apple as the man to save the company was drastically cleaning up the product portfolio.

The visualization of your product line

In order to create a clear and understandable product line, you best plot yourself a visual representation of it. This allows you to analyze the logic and consistency and, when satisfied with the results, use it to inform the rest of the company.

- Visualize the products in the line along two axes: pricing and feature-richness for instance. Each product is characterized by its main features or added features (compared with the cheaper product in the line). Try also to create one discriminating headline for each product.

- Create first the internal positioning chart. This chart will reflect the internal goals and characteristics. Is the product the money-maker? Is it the technology show-off? Is it the price-breaker, with the intention to up-sell?

- Create a positioning chart for the external positioning, listing the customer characteristics, product characteristic and other relevant positioning information.

- Check the pricing differences, the deltas, from product to product within the same product line. Does the difference in pricing make sense? Is it consistent?

Always try to look at the product line, the differences in features, targeting and pricing from the customer's perspective.

Example: Figure 13.10 is an example of how you can simply visualize the internal positioning. The software company Garden-Help, introduced in Chapter 6, now has a product line of three products: Garden-Lite, Garden-Pro and Garden-Pro Enterprise:

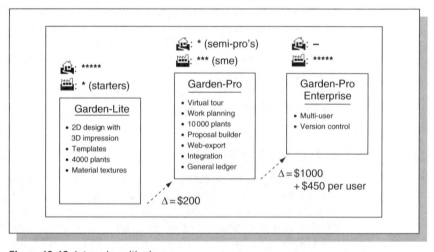

Figure 13.10 Internal positioning

Conclusions

The marketing and marketing planning of a product cannot be separated from the other products in the product portfolio. A well-balanced portfolio of products contains newly introduced products (the question marks), products that create a lot of attention (the stars) and products that generate the cash to fund the marketing of the question marks and the stars (the cash cows).

By plotting out the products in a diagram, such as the BCG's growth/share matrix or the General Electric/McKinsey nine-cell matrix, helps you to foresee problems and define your portfolio strategy.

The internal positioning of products within a product family or line of products is needed to maximize the overall revenue, helps customers to select their ideal product and helps sales to 'sell-up' from an entry-level product to a more feature-rich product.

Interesting links on the web

http://www.themanager.org/Models/BostonBox.htm
http://www.quickmba.com/strategy/matrix/bcg
http://www.marketingteacher.com/Lessons/lesson_boston_
%20matrix.htm
http://www.bcg.com/this_is_bcg/mission/growth_share_matrix.jsp
http://www.quickmba.com/strategy/matrix/ge-mckinsey

The product plan

Many references in this book has been made to the product plan. This appendix shows you the possible table of contents for your product plan, plus some hints and tips for the content itself.

All the information you gathered for the design of your product should be written down in your product plan, from the vision and product mission statement to the market research and target market to the product definition, the forecasting and the financial paragraph.

1 Management Summary
- Short introduction about the document and its content.
- Positioning statement of the product, summarizing the compelling reason(s) to buy, the target market segment, the USPs and how it compares to competing products.
- The expected revenue and the contribution.
- The investments and time needed to develop and introduce the product.

Try to limit the size of the management summary to one or two pages.

2 The Product

2.1 Background and goals
This paragraph reflects the vision behind the product, the basic idea for the product and the high-level goals.

2.2 The product definition
The product definition will vary from product to product; try to make a logical division in paragraphs, for instance:
2.2.1 Standard features and their benefits
2.2.2 Optional features and their benefits
2.2.3 Configurations
2.2.4 Hardware requirements
2.2.5 Software requirements.

2.3 The unique selling points
List the USPs and explain the uniqueness, focusing on the benefits.

2.4 Cost calculation
You have done your cost price analysis (see Chapter 8) and explain, if necessary, the choices you have made.

2.5 Pricing
Explain your pricing strategy and the pricing models for standard configurations, possible options, reseller discounts and other pricing-related topics. Your pricing strategy should contain how your product pricing relates to other products in the market and how it relates to other products in your company's product portfolio.

2.6 Packaging
What are your requirements for packaging your product. Does it come in a full-color box? Will you have manuals on CD-ROM or are they to be printed? Do you have requirements for the size of a box to be able to sit on a shelf space in a store?

These and other considerations and decisions need to be described here. If you can, complete it with a 'bill of materials'.

2.7 Distribution
Describe in this paragraph how your product will be distributed and what distribution channels will be used.

2.8 Installation requirements

3 The Market

3.1 Internal and external analysis (SWOT)

3.2 Market segmentation and targeting

3.3 Competition.

4 Development and Implementation
This chapter contains the planning and roles and responsibilities for the development of the product.

4.1 Technical development

4.2 Development of marketing materials

4.3 Training

4.4 Supporting system, billing requirements and so on.

5 Promotion

5.1 Product positioning statement

5.2 The product launch

5.3 Lead generation.

6 Financials

6.1 Investments needed

6.2 Forecast

6.3 ROI and BEP analysis.

7 Product Lifetime Expectations
This Appendix and Chapter 8 puts your product in a wider perspective. Explain when you expect the end of life of your product and why.

8 Next Releases
You will most likely already have plans for a next release, another product that is a derivative of your

product (for instance targeted at a nice market, a professional version) and in this chapter you can briefly explain these plans and the timeline: the product roadmap. A graphical representation of your product roadmap is preferable.

Product marketing industry benchmark 2003

The text below is, with permission, copied (without modifications) from www.productmarketing.com/magazine/2/1/2003survey.htm

The survey is conducted by Steve Johnson and gives you an adequate profile of today's product managers in the technology industry.

**Product Management Roles & Salary
Industry Compensation Benchmark
for 2003**

Steve Johnson
December 2003
sjohnson@pragmaticmarketing.com

Each year Pragmatic Marketing conducts a survey of product managers, marketing managers, and other marketing professionals. Our objective is to provide Pragmatic Marketing clients with industry information about compensation as well as the most common responsibilities for product managers and other marketing professionals.

The survey was mailed to 5000 marketing professionals with 560 responses.

The survey was conducted during the period of November 25–30, 2003 using WebSurveyor.

Profile of a product manager

The average Product Manager is 36 years old;
84% claim to be "somewhat" or "very" technical;
94% have completed college, 56% have some MBA
    classes, and 47% have completed a masters program;
30% are female, 70% are male.

The typical product manager has responsibility for three
    products.

Organization

The typical product manager reports to a director in the marketing department.

- 43% report to a director
- 33% to VP
- 27% report directly to the CEO
- 23% are in the Marketing department
- 15% are in Development or Engineering
- 10% are in the Product Management department
- 10% are in a sales department

Impacts on Productivity

Product managers receive 65 emails a day and send about 33.

Product managers spend roughly two days a week in internal meetings (14 meetings/week).
But 30% are going to 15 meetings or more each week and 25% attend 19 or more meetings!

Working with requirements

The majority of product managers are researching market needs, writing requirements, and monitoring development projects.

- 72% researching market needs
- 55% preparing business case
- 24% performing win/loss analysis
- 85% monitoring development projects
- 79% writing requirements
- 50% writing specifications

Working with marcom and sales

Product managers also spend time providing technical content for marcom and sales.

- 49% writing promotional copy
- 38% proofing promotional communications
- 38% talking to press and analysts
- 53% training sales people
- 35% going on sales calls

Compensation

Average product management compensation is
$91,650 salary
plus **$11,363** annual bonus
(as in 2002, 78% of product managers get a bonus)

Regional impact on compensation

Compensation (in US$)	Female			Male			Overall		
	Salary	Bonus	Total	Salary	Bonus	Total	Salary	Bonus	Total
Mid Atlantic	$85,154	$10,900	$96,054	$92,278	$10,286	$102,563	$89,290	$10,542	$99,832
Midwest	75,941	6,818	82,759	82,404	11,649	94,053	80,688	10,542	91,229
North East	87,600	15,625	103,225	99,070	12,194	111,264	94,853	13,250	108,103
Pacific Northwest	86,667	4,000	90,667	87,563	7,333	94,896	87,421	6,857	94,278
South	83,100	12,000	95,100	89,647	11,174	100,821	88,159	11,367	99,526
Southwest	93,250	9,200	102,450	83,333	11,250	94,583	86,783	10,647	97,430
West Coast	90,452	6,421	96,873	106,571	14,537	121,108	101,255	11,967	113,222
US Average	$86,252	$9,914	$96,167	$94,097	$11,943	$106,040	$91,650	$11,363	$103,013
Canada (in US$)	77,556	3,500	81,056	74,750	12,500	87,250	75,432	11,115	86,548
Canada (in CN$)	$102,916	$4,645	$107,561	$99,193	$16,588	$115,781	$100,099	$14,750	$114,849

Our bonuses are based on:

- 57% company profit
- 30% product revenue
- 42% quarterly objectives (MBOs)

Almost 40% say the **bonus does not motivate** at all and only 10% say the bonus motivates a lot.

What should the company know about the role of product management?

- PM role is more strategic than tactical
- I don't have time to do all that I can contribute strategically
- We tend to be understaffed
- Product management is not sales support
- I need to visit the market to be a good product manager

Product Management ratios within the company

How are product managers allocated relative to other departments?
For each Product Manager (PM), we find:

- 2.7 Products
- 0.7 Product Lines
- 1.0 Services
- 13.3 Developers
- 1.7 Development Leads
- 1.7 Sales Engineers/Pre-sales support
- 5.0 Sales people

For companies with both product managers and product marketing managers, the average is 3.82 product managers and 2.63 product marketing managers for 13.84 products.

Product management technology environment

Product managers use a fairly standard computing setup, usually a laptop running Office XP, with these operating system characteristics:

- Windows XP (50%) or Windows 2000 Professional (37%)
- Internet Explorer (95%)
- 1024 × 768 screen resolution or better (87%)
- Cookies enabled (98%)
- Java enabled (98%)
- Plug ins installed
  - Shockwave Flash (94%)
  - Adobe Acrobat [PDF] (72%)
  - Java plug-in (63%) (updated April 2004)

Index